The IEA Health and Welfare Unit

Choice in Welfare No. 14

God and the Marketplace

The IEA Health and Welfare Unit

Choice in Welfare No. 14

God and the Marketplace

Essays on the Morality of Wealth Creation

Jon Davies (Editor)

Michael Novak
Bishop John Jukes
Rev Dr Simon Robinson
Richard H. Roberts
Rev John Kennedy
Geoff Moore
Rev Dr James Francis
Vin Arthey

IEA Health and Welfare Unit
London, 1993

First published in 1993
by
The IEA Health and Welfare Unit
2 Lord North St
London SW1P 3LB

© The IEA Health and Welfare Unit 1993

All rights reserved

ISBN 0-255 36275-7

Typeset by the IEA Health and Welfare Unit
in Palatino 11 on 12 point
Printed in Great Britain by
Goron Pro-Print Co. Ltd
Churchill Industrial Estate, Lancing, West Sussex

v

Contents

Foreword

Many of the IEA's publications are technical examinations of the functioning of specific markets. But such studies are not the only concern of the Institute. Indeed, its original memorandum of association included among the Institute's objectives the study of the effect of moral factors on the operation of markets. And with good reason, for competitive markets emerged as a central feature of the free societies of the West, so that a full understanding of market competition requires insight into the real character of the freedom we celebrate as the core Western ideal. Among the major influences on the development of Western civilisation has been Christianity, yet it receives scant attention from modern economists.

A paper on *God and the Marketplace* is thus both timely and in the mainstream of the IEA's educational work. Neglect of moral issues has reinforced the tendency of the churches to view markets with suspicion, if not outright hostility. During the Thatcher years when successive administrations, with solid popular backing, sought to abandon collectivism and restore liberty in Britain, the churches typically withheld their blessing, implying that market competition was at best morally dubious, and possibly wicked. Partly because of this attitude, it has become common to describe the Thatcher years as an epoch of greed.

It is a little-known fact that Hayek proposed to the opening meeting of the Mont Pelerin Society that it be called the Acton-Tocqueville Society. The meeting had been called in 1947 because Hayek felt that at the end of a destructive war fought to protect freedom from fascism, opinion leaders in the West had lost sight of the true character of the ideal for which their compatriots had fought and died. Initially a safe haven for beleaguered liberal intellectuals, the annual meetings of the Mont Pelerin Society were soon to become the focal point for scholars from every corner of the globe who sought to understand the tradition of freedom which made Western civilisation worth dying for.

During his opening address at Mont Pelerin, Hayek itemised his priorities for discussion and ventured the view that unless the breach between 'true liberal' ideals and 'religious convictions' could be healed there was 'no hope for a revival of liberal forces'. As it has turned out, the gulf between the churches and enthusiasts for liberty remains as wide today as it was when Hayek spoke. And for this reason we have brought together church leaders, theologians and other academics representing the Anglican, Roman Catholic and Methodist churches to discuss *God and the Marketplace*. If Hayek was right, then liberty will not be safe until the churches and the champions of freedom can resolve their fundamental differences, and it is our hope that this book will make some small contribution to raising mutual understanding.

Finally, may I thank the University of Newcastle upon Tyne for hosting the conference at which the original versions of these papers were presented. Special thanks must go to the Head of the Religious Studies Department, Jon Davies, who organised the conference and edited this collection. Without his diligent efforts the project would not have reached fruition so quickly.

David G. Green

The Authors

Jon Davies is the Head of Department of Religious Studies at the University of Newcastle upon Tyne.

Michael Novak is a theologian who is currently the holder of the George Frederick Jewett Chair in Religion and Public Policy at the American Enterprise Institute in Washington D.C.

The Rt. Revd. John Jukes is the Roman Catholic Bishop of Strathearn and Auxiliary in Southwark.

Simon Robinson is the Anglican Chaplain at the University of Leeds.

Richard Roberts is the Professor of Divinity and Director of the Institute for Religion and the Human Sciences at the University of Saint Andrews.

John Kennedy is Secretary of the Division of Social Responsibility of the Methodist Church.

Geoff Moore is Principal Lecturer at Newcastle Business School, a part of the University of Northumbria at Newcastle (formerly Newcastle Polytechnic). He is a Lay Reader in the Diocese of Durham.

Rev Dr James Francis is Adviser to the Bishop of Durham on Non-Stipendiary Ministry.

Vin Arthey is Executive Producer for Religious Programmes at Tyne Tees Television.

Introduction

Jon Davies

'It is Socialism, not God that has died.' Discuss.

This apocryphal examination question might well have elicited an appreciative reply from Pope Leo XIII. In 1891 he issued '*Rerum Novarum (of New or Revolutionary Things), an Encyclical on the Condition of the Working Classes*'. Forty or so years earlier in 1848 Marx and Engels had issued the *Communist Manifesto*, also concerned with the condition of the working classes—and indeed in some sense sharing with the Pope at least a diagnosis of the problem. Leo XIII referred to new forms of industrial organisation which had produced a society of 'immense wealth for a small number and deepest poverty for the multitude...who lived under a yoke little better than that of slavery itself'.[1] Marx and Engels also insisted that the new epoch had split society 'into two hostile camps, two great classes directly facing each other: Bourgeoisie and Proletariat'.[2] Both Catholic and Communist authors predicted an outcome of the conflict between these two classes—although on this they had very different expectations. Marx and Engels, in a famous phrase, described the bourgeoisie as its own grave-digger, with 'its fall and the victory of the proletariat equally inevitable'.[3] The Pope asserted that such a socialist end to the conflict would harm the individual, families, society and the state, that it was 'a great mistake to imagine that class is spontaneously hostile to class',[4] and that 'socialism is of no use to the workers'.[5]

It is of course true that Pope Leo XIII was almost as dismissive of liberalism as he was of socialism, and at least one of our contributors, John Kennedy, is of the view that this distrust of the progressive elements of the new order left the Roman Catholic Church rather inclined to be too uncritical of the twentieth century totalitarianisms of the Right. This is a long and complex issue: but with the benefit of hindsight, and in the light of the changes in Eastern Europe, it is perhaps reasonable to see the twentieth Century as being in large measure a prolonged experiment in which the two theories of capitalism and socialism have been put to serious and often bloody test. On the European continent at least the issue has been decided in favour of capitalism. For many in the West, and not only for socialists the revelations of the industrial and economic incompetence of Eastern European socialist governments and states, the undermining of social and family life by overt and covert police, spy and terrorist activity, and the decadence and corruption of the ruling elites in these societies has forced a painful recognition of the fact that on practically every count the admonitory predictions of Leo XIII have turned out to be true. For those in the West who always said 'we told you so', the world has changed in their favour and they face not the depressing collapse of misguided and lost optimism but the more complex task of being both properly enthused with legitimate triumph and of having to face up to the fact that the capitalist system has within itself some serious economic and social problems, including the possibility that the initial diagnosis of class tensions presented by Leo XIII may be re-introducing itself, this time organised on a genuinely global scale. On the global scale there may indeed be problems of which neither the authors of *Rerum Novarum* nor the *Communist Manifesto* could possibly be aware and of which and for which we may neither have now nor are likely ever to have solutions. Be that as it may, there are few now in Europe who would advance 'socialism' as the best way of dealing with the problems of the next century.

It is not, clearly, quite so straightforward to take the next step of asserting that capitalism is the best way of dealing with those problems, especially when its manifest and ubiquitous market freedoms seem so corrosive of traditional values in business practices, sexual relationships and inter-generational relationships in the family. It must be noted that neither in *Rerum Novarum* nor in its successor *Centesimus Annus*[6] are there to be found wholesale commendations of capitalism on a par with the wholesale denunciations of socialism! Those theologians who seek to apply the words of God to activities in the market and the economy, and those ordinary men and women who seek in their day-to-day life as buyers and sellers of goods and services to find guidance in those words, live in a world in which traditional Church teaching on economic matters has and continues to have a distinct ambivalence at its core. This is in part because capitalism (like its mirror image socialism) shared in the Enlightenment secular belief in Progress and the perfectibility of man through his own agency. Committed religious thought sees little in either sacred text or in human example to support such a proposition. Related (rather paradoxically) to this is a religious unease with the 'rough and ready' common sense of capitalism, which accepts that it isn't perfect, nor even the best, but merely the least worst of all known human systems: the 'casualties' which are accepted by such an attitude are unacceptable to a religion which has as its radically restless centre Jesus' statement that whatever happens to the least of us happens also to him.

Christianity does not believe that perfection can be expected from man-made this-worldly systems, but neither does it allow that a this-worldly system can be beyond criticism when it fails to be perfect in failing to answer the needs of all men, treated as of equal value! These seemingly irreconcilable positions have one common function: they maintain religious thought in a state of permanent watchful wariness of all social and economic systems.

In a sense this didn't matter as long as the Christian churches could maintain an even-handedness in their distance from both of the main contenders for man's political soul, i.e. capitalism and communism. Such even-handness was rendered impossible by the unpredicted withdrawal of one of the contenders from the contest.

4

That left religion with the task of working out what it really thought of the remaining, and clearly triumphant direction. Pope John Paul's encyclical *Centesimus Annus* invites us to look forward to the next millennium of the Christian era in that light.

In July 1992 a group of distinguished theologians and social theorists gathered at the University of Newcastle upon Tyne and addressed a Conference on God and the Market Place. The Conference was organised jointly by the Institute of Economic Affairs and the Department of Religious Studies at the University, with financial support from the IEA, the University, and Tyne Tees Television. This publication was made possible by generous support from the University's Small Grants Committee, to whom the editor expresses his gratitude.

Eight of the papers presented at that conference are presented here. The 'key note' speaker was Michael Novak, author of *The Spirit of Democratic Capitalism* (published in this country by the IEA, in 1991). Michael Novak's explicit aim is to provide a 'theology for Capitalism', and in the first of our papers he presents his 'Eight arguments about the morality of the marketplace', dealing in particular with the problem of the poor—better addressed, he concludes, under a market and democratic system than under any other. In the second paper in this section the Right Reverend John Jukes, a Roman Catholic Bishop, provides an extended commentary on Christianity and wealth creation. Simon Robinson, Anglican Chaplain at the University of Leeds, provides a detailed comparison of Novak and R.H. Tawney; while the fourth paper, by Professor Richard Roberts of St Andrew's University deals explicitly with Michael Novak's thesis. Richard Roberts is of the view that Novak does not go far enough in radicalizing Christian teaching on what he calls 'the human right to economic creativity'.

In the second section, John Kennedy of the Methodist Church argues that it is 'a crucial part of the calling of the Church to understand what the best political context for the market might be', and the other three papers are attempts to address that issue by people actively trying to carry out such a 'vocation' with and within the structures of the market. Geoff Moore of the University of Northumbria at Newcastle describes the working of Traidcraft and the Shared Interest Society as they operate in an economic method somewhat 'Beyond Competition'. Jim Francis, the Bishop of Durham's Adviser for Non-Stipendiary Ministry, reflects upon the experiences of ministry in secular employment—again, a direct engagement of Christian belief and market practice. Our last paper, 'Selling God—A job for Commercial Television?', by Vin Arthey, Executive Producer, Religious Programmes, Tyne Tees Television is a direct report from the very entrails of capitalism, to use his own phrase. Arthey's paper was presented as an 'after-dinner speech', and proved so provocative and interesting that it is included here as representing a very unusual perspective on what may become a major form of religious 'liturgy'—i.e. media religion, commercially oriented, operating in the 'Information Age' discussed below by Michael Novak.

People who leave a busy high street and enter one of our increasingly empty churches will find an almost unnaturally quiet place. In the noisy business of the market in the free and vocal West, quiet itself is radical. Religion has always provided such places, located in but set apart from the productive and useful activities of men and women going about their daily tasks. In Eastern Europe, and under conditions much more immediately dangerous than those we are in, the churches became spaces in which to preserve a sense of perspective, to evaluate what was going on, and to organise powerful and eventually successful opposition. Similarly, in our society religion offers a place, a space, a tradition, from which to measure the progress of our social and economic system, and to perhaps identify those aspects of our life which are to be accorded a moral status other than that suggested for them by a merely utilitarian calculus. Thus, for example, in a recent IEA publication on the family, *Families without Fatherhood*,[7] the authors took the view that family relationships should be re-endowed with their ancient sacrosanct status, rendered that is as immune as possible from the ebbs and flows of trend, taste, fad

6

and fashion: the task, that is, is to define the boundary of the market, to locate it in moral values which alone can make its 'free' operation possible and which alone can optimise the large and creative competence of the ideas of freedom and individual responsibility.

The Churches now have an historically unique and serious task: to provide a morality *for* a world economic system—and a morality *for* is not the same as an ideology *of*. Churches—the church, or religion, or religions—are the place or places from which this can be done: and this volume is one small offering in that task.

Notes

1   *Rerum Novarum*, Kirwan, Joseph, (ed), CTS 1983, pp. 1-2.

2   The *Communist Manifesto*, introduction by Taylor, A.J.P., Penguin Classic, 1985, p. 80.

3   *Ibid*, p. 94.

4   Pope Leo XIII, *op. cit.*, p. 10.

5   Pope Leo XIII, *op. cit.*, p. 3.

6   *Centesimus Annus*, Pope John Paul II, CTS., 1991.

7   Dennis, N. and Erdos, G., *Families Without Fatherhood*, London: IEA Health and Welfare Unit, 1992.

Section One:

A Theology For Capitalism?

Eight Arguments about the Morality of the Marketplace

Michael Novak

The purpose of this paper is to discuss eight arguments regarding the morality of markets. Five of them derive from recent discussions in Britain, two from Pope John Paul II—and I throw in one for good measure on my own.

Perhaps giving a name to each of these arguments will be useful. The names of the first five are the argument from covetousness; the epistemic argument; the argument from autonomy; the argument from the growing immateriality of preferences; and the argument from the manifest discontents of materialism.

The two arguments from Pope John Paul II are the arguments from creativity and from community. The eighth and final argument is from universal opportunity—that is, the liberation of the poor.

I conclude with a section on the ambiguities of markets.

The First Five Arguments

'The driving power of capitalism,' writes the distinguished English Christian missionary to India, Lesslie Newbigin, 'is the desire of the individual to better his material condition.... The name the New Testament gives to the force in question is covetousness. The capitalist system is powered by the unremitting stimulation of covetousness.'[1]

This is one justification (condemnation, rather) of capitalism. If it were accepted by a poor nation, such a theory would be its own punishment.

Note, too, its image of wealth. Desiring to improve one's material condition is covetousness because whatever one needs for self-improvement already belongs to others. (It is theirs, and one covets it.) But this is to imagine wealth as a fixed sum, all of it previously assigned, and to overlook the dimension of invention, discovery and the creation of new wealth. It is to imagine all gaining of wealth as 'taking.'

Lesslie Newbigin's view of capitalism as covetousness is one example of a Christian interpretation of capitalism. Bishop Richard Harries of Oxford offers a view far more sympathetic, nuanced, and yet detached. His title asks, *Is there a Gospel for the Rich?* and his answer is his 'conviction that God's liberation is for everyone. The rich need to be liberated no less than the poor.'[2] Intelligently and with discrimination, the good bishop discerns Christian potential in the social device of the free market, in private property, in innovation, in the business firm, in profit, and even in the transnational corporation. The *bête-noire* and polemical foil for his book is the New Right, to which he wishes to supply a sophisticated alternative. He describes Britain as a 'post-socialist' society. His aim is to present a more humane and evangelical form of capitalism than any (he thinks) yet dreamed of on the New Right. He is rather bigger on 'affirmative government' than is the New Right, for example.

In offering his argument on behalf of a market economy, Bishop Harries begins with a leader from *The Guardian* in 1981 which accepted the market as an inescapable fact of life and an important source of much needed knowledge: 'It is the market which acts as an essential signal from consumers to firms telling them how much to produce, when to produce it, and what sort of quality to make.' Besides this information, 'the profit of corporations (or cooperatives) is also the market's way of signalling success: it is an essential guide to, and source of, investment.' In brief, Harries summarizes, to all except a very small percentage of the Labour Party the free market is 'essential, inescapable and, for all its flaws, to be valued.'[3] This approval for markets, Harries notes, is 'as robust as could come from any Thatcherite economist.' John Gray calls such a defense of the market the epistemic argument for markets and offers a brief and elegant statement of it in *The Moral Foundations of Market Institutions*.[4]

But Gray also offers another fundamental and at least partly original argument—from autonomy. More than any other system, he argues, a market system enhances the individual's scope for and frequency of acts of choice. Gray does not see this argument as necessarily universal. It may mean less to East Asian societies, for example, whose social and psychological structure is more communitarian, less individualist, than to those of the West. Nor does he think of an emphasis on choice as an unmixed blessing. On this as other things, individuals and societies can go over the top. *What* is chosen can matter greatly. Nonetheless, the argument from autonomy is difficult for any Western intellectual to dismiss, since the Western public values choice highly. The best rejoinder from the Left is to suggest that too few people actually possess autonomy in sufficient degree, so that much social (and governmental) effort must be expended in 'equalizing people' through redistribution.[5]

To his credit, Gray resists redistributionist policies. These are in practice doomed to failure and in principle unjust. But he does argue that any society which favors autonomy must, by that very commitment, empower all its citizens to reach some basic level thereof. Gray thinks he has found a way to define this basic desired level through a concept of 'satiable needs.'[6] Yet since poverty is normally taken as a relative measure—by American standards, for example, more than a third of Western Europeans would be living in poverty[7]—I doubt that Gray's efforts in this direction are sustainable. The human spirit is in principle insatiable. The mind is, as Aristotle said, 'in some way all things'—that is, restless until everything is known that can be known. As St. Augustine put it: 'Our hearts are restless, Lord, until they rest in Thee.' The empirical starting place of the religious quest, and of the Jewish and Christian concept of God, lies in the striving of the human spirit for the infinite. Insatiability is part of our nature.

'If only I could have that,' we have often told ourselves, 'I would be satisfied'—only to find that we never are. Autonomy is always like that. We can never get enough of it. Whatever of it we have always runs into limits, often quickly, and we would fain have no such limits; we would wish to be like God. Even kings and princes rail against their too-narrow autonomy. Such is the stuff of a great deal of the best drama in England, the best in the world—not least in that splendid London play, *The Madness of King George III.*

Fourth, there is an argument for the market based upon the growing immateriality of what people are actually willing to buy. Markets depend on people's choices. Kenneth Adams thinks he has discerned an impending switch in consumers' preferences:

> Suppose that our increasing demand is for entertainment, sport, music, theatre, literature and all other areas of human growth: in relationships, in intellectual and aesthetic delight—these will place much smaller demands on materials and energy. Furthermore, as desire grows in those wider, richer, higher areas of human need, it is likely that desire for increase in the material areas will stabilize or decline.[8]

Or, as George Gilder puts an analogous point: the actual physical material of a computer disc for a software program that costs, say $400 (£220) is made of plastic worth about 85 cents (£1); the rest of the value lies in the information coded on it. That is to say, an increasing proportion of production today lies in its spiritual rather than its material components. Industries are becoming cleaner; through miniaturization, physical products are becoming smaller, more powerful, and (usually) cheaper. The full implications of the term 'Information Age' have barely begun to be absorbed by and articulated in theological thought.

The fifth argument for the market—admittedly an odd one—is that the economic plenty produced by market societies has proved conclusively that 'man does not live by bread alone.' The traditional Jewish and Christian predictions about the discontents inherent in materialism have been confirmed. The textual evidence for this lies in university book stores in the sections (usually larger than for those for traditional philosophy and theology) devoted to astrology, witchcraft, the occult, and New Age religiosity. 'When humans stop believing in God,' Chesterton once wrote, 'they don't believe in nothing; they believe anything.' All around us we see signs of boredom, restlessness, and discontent.

In this our present material paradise, even the poorest pauper has better health care through the National Health Service than poor, mad, blistered, bled, and purgated George III received from the chief of the Royal College of Medicine. Today's busman drives a personal automobile Henry V would have envied. A clerk or porter today has his pick of fresh and varied foods from every tropical and temperate clime on earth. And scurvy, rickets, consumption, smallpox, and other scourges of the poor have all but disappeared. Yet even in this material paradise, our hearts are restless. This is no small gain for market societies to have produced. Whether we can take advantage of it, and inspire new perspectives, is another question.

Plus Two: Arguments from Creativity and Community

None of these five arguments (except perhaps the first) is alien to Pope John Paul II who, as the hundredth anniversary of *Rerum Novarum* approached, was asked again and again by bishops from Sri Lanka to Sao Paulo to Kiev, 'What direction do you now recommend to us, after the collapse of socialism?' The Pope was certain to issue an encyclical commemorating that of his predecessor, so after the events of 1989 he had to provide an answer. He recommended 'the free economy, the market economy,' the economy of creativity and enterprise. He was even willing, although reluctant, to use the word 'capitalism,' so long as the system intended by that word included a worthy juridical system protecting human rights and a moral/religious system imposing ethical limits.[9] Yet his arguments for this decision are rather different from the five preceding arguments.

Pope John Paul II's argument from creativity flows from his concept of 'the acting person,' worked out in his book by that title written before he became Pope.[10] (At that time, however, he had not seen its relevance for economics.) What makes humans distinctive among the other animals, he held, is their capacity to initiate new projects (especially life projects); that is, to imagine, to create, and to *act*, as distinct from merely behaving. Throughout his pontificate, the Pope has focused on this 'creative subjectivity' of the human person.[11] In this he saw the *Imago Dei*: humans made in the image of the Creator, in such a way that to be creative is the essential human vocation. In this, too, he saw the endowment of a fundamental human right to personal economic initiative.

This argument, it will be noted, offers a different grounding for an expression such as 'natural rights' from that offered by Hobbes, Locke, or other Enlightenment figures. The Pope's argument is, in the main, a philosophical argument, and could perhaps be supported by philosophical thought in the manner of Gabriel Marcel, in *The Mystery of Being, Creative Fidelity*, and other books.[12] The emphasis of certain phenomenologists and existentialists on human 'becoming,' on 'creating oneself,' and the like, are other indications of what might be done. This argument also has much to commend it from the viewpoint of commonsense. It is far harder to predict the future of one's children, for example, than that of the household cat. The latter does not have to think about choosing a career at all, let alone to choose among self-invented possibilities. The exact way in which the Pope deploys the argument, of course, depends on the doctrine of creation and a long Christian tradition of interpreting the Book of Genesis. The Pope's is more properly a theological than a philosophical argument. Still, it is quite striking.

The Pope sees that for much of Christian history the most important form of wealth was land, just as the term 'capital' derived from counting the heads (*capita*) of sheep, oxen, cows, goats, horses and other livestock that marked a farm's productivity, along with fruits, vegetables, and grain.[13] Grateful emperors and kings gave out lands as rewards for meritorious service, such as the grant of Blenheim to the Duke of Marlborough by Queen Anne, and many other grants by the Spanish and Portuguese rulers to *conquistadores* in the New World. Wealth in land belonged chiefly to the nobility, although in some places smaller freeholds were also conspicuous, especially in Britain and for unusually long and uninterrupted family tenure. (To this happy accident of history, due in part to Britain's relative safety from invasion by land, both Adam Smith and Max Weber attributed Britain's steady growth in liberty, respect for rights, and prosperity.)

At a later period, the Pope notes, wealth (like the term *Das Kapital*) came to be associated with ownership of the means of production—with machinery, factories, and other impersonal aspects. Indeed, in his first social encyclical, even John Paul II had used 'capital' only for impersonal objects, using 'labor' to refer to human persons as factors in production (whatever their economic role).[14] In *Sollicitudo Rei Socialis*, he had already seen clearly enough that even common ownership of the means of production, and certainly state ownership, could not guarantee the humanity of an economic system—neither its capacity to produce wealth nor its capacity to respect 'the fundamental right to personal economic initiative.'[15] *That* right, he saw then (1907), was grounded in the *Imago Dei* imprinted on man's soul.

In *Centesimus Annus*, the Pope carries this line of thought further. The new, deeper, and more telling referent for the word 'capital' is neither land nor the impersonal means of production but, rather, 'the possession of know-how, technology and skill.' The chief cause of the wealth of nations is human wit—discovery, invention, the habit of enterprise, foresight, skill in organization. 'The wealth of the industrialized nations is based much more on this kind of ownership than on natural resources.'[16] 'Indeed, besides the earth, man's principal resource is *man himself*.' And, again: '...today the decisive factor is increasingly *man himself*, that is, his knowledge, especially his scientific knowledge, his capacity for interrelated and compact organization, as well as his ability to perceive the needs of others and to satisfy them.'[17]

It seems to me, after countless re-readings, that the Pope might be thinking in these passages of Japan—that tiny land with hardly any natural resources, almost 100 per cent dependent on overseas sources of energy. Nonetheless, resource-poor Japan is perhaps the wealthiest nation on earth—and in economic terms the most creative. The cause of Japan's wealth cannot be an abundance of natural resources nor even proximity to its major markets; nor can it be argued that its densely packed population (140 million inhabitants crowded onto the one-fourth of Japan's land mass that is habitable) has rendered Japan hopelessly poor, as the theories of contemporary Malthusians will lead one to predict. Instead, the Japanese have highly developed, and make exquisite use of, their human capital. For 130 years, since the Meiji Reforms, Japanese education has been on an admirable upward curve. Without the pressure of the Western cultivation of autonomy, the Japanese capacity for coordination and organization is without peer. If Japanese workers appear to Western eyes to behave more like a willing flock or docile herd than Westerners could bear to behave, nonetheless, they have also shown their ability to emulate the Western, especially the American, zest for discovery, innovation, flexibility, quick response, and competitive drive. Without even recognizing the Creator of whom Pope John Paul II speaks, the Japanese have shown remarkable capacities for creative action in world manufacturing markets. If John Paul II's theory about the *universal* human capacity for creativity is true, then this is as it should be. Creativity by any other name causes wealth, as natural resources alone do not.

But the very powerful communitarian and centripetal structure of Japanese society brings to light the other argument for markets made by Pope John Paul II: that where human creativity is at play today, a new and highly interesting form of community is also at play. In the largest sense, the market of today is a world market; it interknits every part of the world within a single, complex web of contracts, transactions, and networks of supply and demand. Many of these transactions are instantaneous. World markets, both for stock and for commodities, and above all for information (the newest, most vital form of capital), are open for simultaneous viewing on television and computer screens linked to one another around the world in 'real time.'

Dostoevsky once described charity as an invisible filament linking the world in a network of impulses, along which a simple human smile or an aspiration of love could circle the globe in minutes to bring cheer to someone, even a stranger, faraway. A person who receives a smile, he noted, often feels impelled to pass it along by smiling to someone else in the next chance encounter, and so with the speed of light the smile circles the globe. The new television and computer images, like impulses bounced off cold and silent satellites in space to touch and vivify every part of earth, may only be metaphors for the nerves and tissues that have always tied together the Mystical Body spoken of by St. Paul, but such ligatures seem more visible now. Even in the fifth century A.D., a great father of the Church (I believe it was Gregory of Nyssa), observed that human trade, exchanging the wool of one place for the wine of another, the clay pots of one culture for the grain of another, is an image of the bonds uniting the one family of God. Better these links should be visible in voluntary trade than in world war. 'Commercium et Pax' was once (and may be still) the motto of Amsterdam, whose scenes of commerce and shipping were painted often by Turner.

Obviously, though, the Pope's focus is more on the Christian West (and Third World) than on Japan, and I have no idea in fact whether he ever thought of Japan at all. Yet even in the supposedly more individualistic West, the Pope sees that the market is, above all, a social instrument. It has a centripetal force. It obliges sellers to find buyers (sometimes at great distances and across significant spans of time). It calls for sequences of action that involve many different hands coordinated by remarkable capacities for foresight and organization. Indeed, most economic activities in the modern environment are too complex to be executed by one person alone; nearly all of them require the creation of a new type of community, not organic but artifactual, not 'natural' (as the family is natural) but contractual, not coercive (as was 'real existing socialism') but free and voluntary, not total like a monastery but task-oriented and open to cooperators even of diverse belief systems and ultimate commitments. In short, the distinctive invention of capitalist societies is the business firm, independent of the state.

About the business firm, the Pope is surprisingly eloquent. There has been a tendency in Catholic thought (the document of Vatican II on 'The Church in the World,' Oswald Nell-Breuning, S.J., has pointed out,[18] is one example) to notice only four economic roles: the owner, the manager, the employer, and the employee; while neglecting entirely the creative source of the firm, the practitioner of the virtue of enterprise, the entrepreneur. Pope John Paul II does not fall into this pattern. Here is what he writes in *Centesimus Annus*:

> *People work with each other*, sharing in a 'community of work' which embraces ever widening circles. A person who produces something other than for his own use generally does so in order that others may use it after they have paid a just price, mutually agreed upon through free bargaining. It is precisely the ability to foresee both the needs of others and the combinations of productive factors most adapted to satisfying those needs that constitutes another important source of wealth in modern society. Besides, many goods cannot be adequately produced through the work of an isolated individual; they require the cooperation of many people in working towards a common goal. Organizing such a productive effort, planning its duration in time, making sure that it corresponds in a positive way to the demands which it must satisfy, and taking the necessary risks—all this too is a source of wealth in today's society.

A few lines later the Pope comes back to this theme:

> It is [man's] disciplined work in close collaboration with others that makes possible the creation of ever more extensive *working communities* which can be relied upon to transform man's natural and human environments. Important virtues are involved in this process, such as diligence, industriousness, prudence in undertaking reasonable risks, reliability and fidelity in interpersonal relationships, as well as courage in carrying out decisions which are difficult and painful but necessary, both for the overall working of a business and in meeting possible set-backs.[19]

Contemplating this modern economic process—this historically unique way of drawing upon the creative individual working within voluntary, cooperative community—the Pope writes this quite stunning sentence: 'This process, *which throws practical light on a truth about the human person which Christianity has constantly affirmed*, should be viewed carefully and favorably.' The modern business process—*business*, of all things!—'throws practical light on [Christian] truth.' And then note: the Pope urges theologians and other Christians to view this business process 'carefully and favorably.' The Pope is only exercising here the classic Catholic habit of seeing in all things the signs of Providence at work, the hidden presence of that Logos 'by whom and with whom and in whom were made all the things that are made.' (John 1:1-3). Sometimes referred to as the Catholic 'sacramental sense' or 'way of analogy,' this mode of perception lies behind the tradition of blessing the fishing fleets, the fields to be sown, and the harvests. If humans are made in the image of God, then their actions (especially their creative actions) are also so marked. As Georges Bernanos wrote at the end of *The Diary of a Country Priest*, 'Grace is everywhere.'[20] Even William Butler Yeats took up the sentiment: 'Everything I look upon is blest.'

It is remarkable, of course, that something so scorned in literature as the business firm and the modern corporation should be set before us by a Catholic Pope, as a lesson to 'be viewed carefully and favorably' for the 'practical light' it sheds on Christian truth. (I personally know writers who, if I had written that line, would have described it as excessive.) Yet such praise fits quite comfortably within an old tradition, in whose light grace was seen to be working even in rather tyrannical and amoral kings; in the thief who died beside Jesus on the cross; and in every neighbor a man meets. To see grace at work is not to see only beauty and light, but real things as they are, in this messy, fleshly, and imperfect world. For the Creator looked on this world and proclaimed it 'good,' and for its redemption He gave His only Son. A Catholic is taught to see grace in flawed and all-too-human popes, in the poor of Calcutta, and (hardest of all sometimes) in himself.

In summary, the Pope has advanced two new arguments in support of his proposal that market systems shed practical light on Christian truth, and advance human welfare. The first is that markets give expression to the creative subjectivity of the human person, who has been created in the image of the Creator of all things, and called to help complete the work of creation through sustained, historical effort.

His second argument is that markets generate new and important kinds of community, while expressing the social nature of human beings in rich and complex ways. Markets are not in their essence instruments of alienation, exploitation, anarchy, and centrifugal egoism. They are good instruments that serve human community. Like all things human, however, they can be used inadequately, badly, and for evil purposes. No less than man himself are they capable of both good and evil. Yet to concede that markets are in themselves good is to concede a great deal. To recommend them merely as better than any known alternative is to praise them quite sufficiently.

And One for Good Measure

To add my own voice to that of the Pope may seem impertinent; yet it is the duty of theologians to attack advance outposts and to scout unsettled lands. So I wish to propose another reason for proposing markets as a strategy of a Christian theology of liberation for the poor; viz., a proposition for which the evidence of immigration patterns around the world offers *prima facie* support: that market systems better allow the poor to rise out of poverty than any other known social system. Economic opportunity on this planet is as scarce as oil. Immigrants stream towards it by the million.

Great Britain, Canada, Germany, Italy—most of the market systems on this planet receive steady streams of immigrants. The United States alone during the 20 years 1970-1990 accepted some 16 million *legal* immigrants. (Nobody knows in addition how many illegal ones came through our porous borders.) This is as if we had accepted during that time a new population four times larger than Switzerland's. Most of these new citizens arrived in America poor. America is quite good at helping immigrants to find opportunity, provided only that the latter are willing to seize it, as the vast majority do. (One should remember this in learning that of the 250 million citizens of the U.S. in 1989, 31 million were counted as poor, for want of an annual income of $13,400 for a family of four.) Most of those new citizens were also nonwhite. Indeed, in our largest state, California, English is now the *second* language of a plurality of households. This is why Americans rank 'opportunity' quite high in evaluating economic systems. Bishop Harries does not quite get this point; he dismisses 'the American dream,' which is in fact more universal than he allows, in peremptory fashion:

> It is not an ignoble [dream] but it is certainly limited. By its nature some fail to make it and are left behind, and when their numbers run into many millions questions must be asked.[21]

Questions must always be asked, but the perspective ought not to be skewed. Although virtually 100 per cent of Americans arrived in America poor, today 87 per cent are not poor, and we must now do better with the remaining 13 per cent. Of these, only about 8 million of America's 30 million officially designated 'poor' persons are able-bodied persons between the ages of 18 and 64; the rest are either 65 or older, or 17 and younger, or sick and disabled. For the 8 million able-bodied, the work of the 'opportunity society' is not yet complete.[22]

America is also good at helping most of the American-born poor—the elderly, those under 18, the sick, and the disabled—for whom economic opportunity is not a saving option. Where private family care is not available to them, where the many programs of civil society let them down, government medical aid, food stamps, housing assistance and other programs have been supplied to fill the gap. This is good and proper. Particularly for the elderly, the 'war on poverty' launched in the mid-1960s was a great success. Millions are living far longer and at a higher standard of well-being than ever before. The 'elderly' (those over 85) have supplanted those over 65 as the major concern.

But for younger adults in good health, the 'war on poverty' has actually done much damage.[23] Our government programs have failed our young. The fastest growing group among the poor has been single female householders with young children. This did not happen before, when people were far poorer than at present, and when current government programs barely existed. Never before have so many males deserted females through separation, divorce, or the generation of children out of wedlock, with little or no sense of paternal responsibility. The results have been deplorable for children, the young mothers and the young males themselves.

Thus, the great moral and social problem facing the United States today is to devise new ways to help this group of 8-10 million able-bodied poor adults, mostly young, in ways that do not reduce them to a kind of serfdom, and further depress their morale. On ways to reform recent practices, I have elsewhere written (with a team of others) at much greater length.[24]

Here I want to stress, rather, the crucial importance of dynamic market systems for raising up the poor of Central and Eastern Europe, Latin America, and throughout the Third World (which is actually several quite different worlds). For what these poor millions—some 2.5 billion of them—have in common is not only a lack of opportunity but a sustained, systematic repression of their right to personal economic initiative. Most of them find in their homelands no institutions that might nourish and support that right: constitutionally protected private property, open markets, cheap and easy legal incorporation of businesses, access to legal and low-cost credit, technical assistance, training, and the like. To gain access to such institutions many millions must seek freedom of opportunity far from home.

Throughout the Third World it is important that it soon becomes cheap, easy, and quick for poor people to incorporate small businesses. Latin American systems are patrimonial; although these nations have markets, private property, and profit (in the precapitalist way), small elites still control the apparatus of the state, and thus still control access to the economy. Most Latin American nations are not opportunity societies. Opportunity is the great comparative advantage—much more important than 'natural resources'—that the U.S. has over its Latin American neighbors. To seek opportunity, many Latinos must migrate northwards.

The fact that market systems open opportunity for the poor is one of the most important arguments in their favor. I mean, of course, the type of market economy that is not protective of the rich but gives the able-bodied poor many opportunities. Such markets, regularly revolutionized by new inventions and new technologies, bring down many of the formerly rich (as old technologies and ossified firms become obsolete). Similarly, they raise up many of the formerly poor (as new inventions and new forms of knowledge generate new opportunities). But their greatest strength lies in the openness and dynamism of the small business sector, through which so many millions rise out of poverty.

Open markets liberate the poor better than any known alternative. Open markets favor creativity and dynamism. They also narrow the perceived distance between personal action and personal fate. And to narrow that gap is to strengthen human dignity.[25] The experience of that dignity makes free peoples walk with a confident gait and evenness of eye.

The peoples of the whole world should have the opportunity to walk that walk, as now most of them do not. That is why systemic change is necessary in the Third World. Market systems allow human creativity freedom to act. Nonetheless, like all things human, market systems are not without their ambiguities.

The Ambiguities of Markets

One of my favorite writers on social ethics in Britain is Ronald H. Preston of Scotland, a follower of the great American theologian of the last generation, Reinhold Niebuhr. Preston's latest book *Religion and the Ambiguities of Capitalism* fits comfortably in the sequence of R.H. Tawney's *Religion and the Rise of Capitalism*, V.A. Demant's *Religion and the Decline of Capitalism*, and his own *Religion and the*

Persistence of Capitalism.[26] (The sequence of these titles, by authors who consider themselves friends of socialism rather than capitalism, is in itself rather illuminating: from the worrying *rise*, to the comforting *decline*, to the puzzling *persistence*, to the scrupulously discerned *ambiguities* of 'almost triumphant' capitalism.) While fussing about its residual problems, Preston concedes much of the historical argument to capitalism, including its stress on the importance of innovation, incentives, private ownership, flexibility (rather than central planning) with respect to the future, and the many utilities of markets. He reformulates the traditional argument less forthrightly than did the American Marxist writer Robert Heilbroner ('Less than seventy-five years after it officially began the contest between capitalism and socialism is over: capitalism has won.')[27] Preston writes rather more complacently:

> I propose to argue that the issue is not between the free market and the central, planned economy, but how far we can get the best of what the social market and democratic socialist models propose.[28]

Now this proposal is remarkable in two ways: first, it turns out, Preston's discussion of the social market model and the democratic socialist model stresses the virtues of markets to a surprising degree. Second, Preston's own ideological commitments prevent him from even considering what many take to be a more humane, dynamic, progressive, and Christian alternative to social market and democratic socialist economies, viz., the democratic capitalist model; he simply leaves it out of account. Preston is quick to spot ideology in others, writing often of 'ideologists' or 'ideologues' to his Right, while describing himself as a realist. (When he lapses into preaching that 'a positive attitude to taxation is needed among citizens. It is a good thing to pay taxes!', one does doubt his realism.)[29]

More admirably, Preston qualifies his own 'social Christianity' by taking on board some of the insights offered by writers to his Right, such as Nobel prize winners Friedrich Hayek and James M. Buchanan. Moreover (although he seems not to recognize it), many of the arguments he makes concerning the 'ambiguity' of markets are also consistent with the philosophy of democratic capitalism. Among these are such arguments as these: that 'we cannot do without markets, nor can we do with them alone;'[30] that markets 'have to be rigorously monitored to prevent the creation of cartels, quotas, monopolies and other restrictions'[31] (see Adam Smith); that markets produce inequalities of income, not wholly in accord with inequalities of merit or effort, and thus give rewards at least partly on a pre-moral basis; that markets are not good for all purposes, for example, some public goods; and that there are sometimes externalities for which some agents escape paying proper costs. All these points (and more) are included under what is meant by 'democratic capitalism.'[32] For example, there are some things that should never be bought or sold; in some domains, markets are illegitimate; neither democracy nor the market is a device suited for all purposes, etc. On such matters, Preston and I are in agreement.

Yet there is one point on which Preston seems clearly to be incorrect, at least by omission—his treatment of inequalities of income. First he praises markets for what they do well, as follows:

> To recapitulate, other things being equal, markets are a highly efficient way of getting economic decisions made in accordance with the freedom of choice expressed by consumers: that is, by the dispersed exercise of political and economic power. They are an incentive to thrift and innovation, so tending to maximize the productivity of relatively scarce economic resources.

But then Preston adds a sentiment in need of vigorous challenge:

> On the other hand, left to themselves market economies produce cumulative inequalities of income which distort the market by drawing the relatively scarce resources to what the wealthy want and away from the necessities of the poor.[33]

The assumption here seems to be that noncapitalist systems do this better. But this is clearly not true of the precapitalist Third World regimes of present-day Latin America, Africa, and Asia, in which inequalities of income are of enormous proportions, while for the poor opportunity scarcely exists. Nor is it true of communist societies, whose poor are now known to have lived in unsuspected squalor and whose elites lived in closed circles of high privilege.

Furthermore, Preston omits another salient contrast. Neither precapitalist (traditional) societies nor socialist societies have done much to lift large majorities of their populations out of poverty, as democratic capitalist nations have done. The degree of upward mobility in capitalist societies has no precedent in history, and the array of opportunities they offer to the poor for advancement by way of talent and effort has had no equal. Moreover, it does not seem to be true that market economies produce 'cumulative' inequalities of income, or that these draw 'relatively scarce resources' away from 'the necessities of the poor.'

To begin with the last assertion first, the condition of the poor today is far improved over what it was, say, in 1892 (or 1932), so that the very word 'necessities' now entails far higher standards than in centuries past—far above mere survival or subsistence. The phrase 'relatively scarce resources,' furthermore, is similarly problematic.

Finally, Preston's accusation of 'cumulative' inequalities of income seems doubly dubious. For one thing, during the life cycle of individuals incomes tend to rise and then fall; for another, there is immense churning among individuals moving up and down within income brackets from one decade to another. Again, fortunes are often dissipated within a decade after the death of the accumulator. Technologies on which a fortune may be based become speedily obsolete; heirs are seldom so talented or as highly motivated as the creators of the family fortune. Downward mobility is frequent. Elites circulate with rapidity. Preston seems to take the unilateral, cumulative growth of wealth as a given; the staggering fragility and the changeability of fortunes would seem far more prevalent.

Possibly, this difference in perception is due to the unique fluidity of American social structure, as contrasted with that of Europe. To a remarkable degree, European societies are still ribbed within aristocratic, feudal institutions; the United States is far more committed to universal opportunity and, in that respect is a more purely capitalist society. Quite often in Europe today, dominant firms are still run by the descendants of old aristocratic families.[34] There really is a perception that wealth and power are stable and cumulative. In America, by contrast, the great families of the 1700s have nearly all died out or lost their prominence; with few exceptions, such as the Rockefellers, the same is true of the great families of the 1800s. Many of the great fortunes of today have been acquired by the living; a significant number, especially among the *nouveaux riches* of film and entertainment, have also been lost by the living. Great inequalities there may well be, but these are remarkably ephemeral. In addition, always morally, and often economically, it is not position that counts but quality of performance.

Besides, the good Lord Himself forbade covetousness five times in ten commandments; envy is to be resisted. Equality of income is an ideal appropriate only to the unfree and the uniform. What matters far more than inequality is universal opportunity.[35] As an ideal, universal opportunity is far better suited to creatures made in the image of God, and by God's Providence set in dissimilar circumstances. On this fundamental moral issue, Preston should face more squarely the ambiguities of socialism. He might in that confrontation begin to detect its moral and anthropological errors.

Democracy, capitalism, and pluralism (the three social systems whose combination constitutes democratic capitalism) are, each of them, ambiguous. All things human are. The relevant social question is not: 'Is this utopia?' but rather, 'Compared to what?' In comparing which system is more likely to bring about universal opportunity, prosperity from the bottom up, the *embourgeoisement* of the proletariat, and the raising up of the poor, the historical answer is clear: for the poor, market systems provide far better chances of improving income, condition, and status. That is one reason why so many of the world's poor migrate toward democratic and capitalist systems.

In a word, market systems combined with democratic political systems (protecting the rights of minorities and individuals) offer better hope to the poor of the world than socialist or traditionalist systems do. Despite their inevitable ambiguities, that is one of their strongest claims to moral recognition.

Notes

1   Newbigin, L., *Foolishness to the Greeks*, London: SPCK, 1986, p. 113.

2   Harries, Richard, *Is There a Gospel for the Rich?*, London: Mowbray, 1992, p. 72.

3   *Ibid.*, 88-89.

4   Gray, John, *The Moral Foundations of Market Institutions*, IEA Health and Welfare Unit, Choice in Welfare Series No. 10, London: 1992, pp. 5-17.

5   See *ibid.*, Chapter 4, 'The Mirage of Egalitarianism.'

6   *Ibid.*, Chapter 6, 'An Enabling Welfare State,' pp. 63-72.

7   Rector, Robert, 'How "Poor" Are America's Poor?', Heritage Foundation *Backgrounder* No. 791, September 1990.

8   'Changing British attitudes,' *RSA Journal*, November 1990, referred to by Harries, p. 80.

9   *Centesimus Annus*, #42.

10 Wojtyla, Karol, *The Acting Person*, trans. Potocki, Andrzej, Boston: D. Reidel, 1979; Originally published as *Osobai czyn*, Dordrecht, 1969.

11 *Sollicitudo Rei Socialis*, #15.

12 Marcel, Gabriel, *Creative Fidelity*, New York: Farrar, Strauss and Company, 1964; *The Mystery of Being*, Chicago: Gateway Edition, 1960.

13 *Centesimus Annus*, #32.

14 *Laborem Exercens*.

15 *Sollicitudo Rei Socialis*, #15.

16 *Centesimus Annus*, #32

17 *Ibid.*

18 Nell-Breuning, Oswald, *Commentary on the Documents of Vatican II*, vol. 5, New York: Herder and Herder, 1969, p. 299.

19 *Centesimus Annus*.

20 See the final lines of the novel by George Bernanos, *Diary of a Country Priest*, trans. Pamela Morris, New York: Macmillan, 1962.

21 Harries, p. 101. Harries sometimes writes as if most of the poor in America were black or Hispanic (actually nearly three-fourths are white) and as if a majority of blacks and Hispanics were poor (actually about two-thirds of each are not poor). The single greatest determinant of poverty is not race but belonging to a household headed by a single mother.

22 In totting up who is poor, the U.S. Census Bureau does not count such welfare benefits as medical care, housing, food stamps or, in general, noncash assistance, for all of which the poor are eligible.

23 Murray, Charles, *Losing Ground*, New York: Basic Books, 1984.

24 Novak, Michael, *et al.*, *New Consensus on Family and Welfare*, Washington, D.C.: American Enterprise Institute for Public Policy Research, 1987 and Milwaukee: Marquette University, 1987.

25 No human agency can narrow that gap to zero, since luck and circumstance are powerful winds of fortune. But even to narrow that gap is to strengthen human dignity.

26 Preston, Ronald H., *Religion and the Ambiguities of Capitalism*, London: SCM Press, 1991; Tawney, R.H., *Religion and the Rise of Capitalism*, Harmondsworth, Middlesex, England: Penguin Books, 1964; Demant, V.A., *Religion and the Decline of Capitalism*, Excelsior, Minnesota: Melvin McCosh Bookseller, 1952 and Preston, Ronald H., *Religion and the Persistence of Capitalism*, Philadelphia: Trinity Press International, 1979.

27 Heilbroner, Robert L., 'The Triumph of Capitalism', *The New Yorker*, January 23, 1989.

28 Preston, *Religion and the Ambiguities of Capitalism*, p. 15.

29 *Ibid.*, p. 75.

30 *Ibid.*

31 *Ibid.*

32 See, e.g., my *The Spirit of Democratic Capitalism*, London: IEA, 1991, 1st ed., 1982; *Catholic Social Thought and Liberal Institutions*, New Brunswick, New Jersey: Transaction Publishers, 1989, 1st ed., 1984 and *Will It Liberate?*, Lanham, Maryland: Madison Books, 1991, 1st ed., 1986; *Free Persons and the Common Good*, Lanham, Md.: Madison Books, 1990; *This Hemisphere of Liberty*, Lanham, Md.: Madison Books, 1991.

33 Preston, p. 74.

34 Buttiglione, Rocco, 'Christian Economics 101,' *Crisis*, July-August, 1992: p. 34.

35 The study group cited *supra*, n. 24, discerned six criteria or goals that the good society must meet with respect to the poor. The group presupposed continuing economic growth: 'Not long ago poverty meant living just above subsistence. By now it means a level of basic decency, and this level is expected to rise slowly with the times.' The six criteria are:

- Decade by decade, the proportions of the poor ought to be reduced.
- Decade by decade, the standard of expectable necessities required for a decent standard of living should rise. This includes such mundane measures as household appliances and living space, but also such important measures as higher standards of longevity, of infant mortality, and of health.
- Every able-bodied poor person ought to have the opportunity to exit from poverty. If the poverty of some is persistent, or if it persists among particular groups over long periods, something seems seriously wrong.
- Those of the poor unable to exit from poverty, through no fault of their own but because of disability, illness, or old age, should find adequate assistance from others, including government as a last resort.
- Those of the poor who can through their own efforts exit from poverty should be able to find the jobs necessary for them to do so.
- Given an open society and personal effort, talent should often emerge (and be rewarded) among persons born poor; and their invention, creativity, and personal liberty should flourish. Thus, the free circulation of individuals in both upward and downward mobility should respond primarily to individual talent, effort, and opportunity.

The New Consensus on Family and Welfare, op cit., p. 7.

Christianity and Wealth Creation
Competition and the Values Demanded by the Christian Gospel

Bishop John Jukes

In keeping with the main theme of this conference I will develop my theme by presenting some reflections upon 'competition' since this is a key element in current economic and social thinking. I cannot find much specific teaching on 'competition' in the official documents of the Catholic church so the views here expressed are largely my own.

The English word *wealth* ordinarily signifies riches, large possessions, opulence, abundance etc., (cf. Concise Oxford English Dictionary etc.). The use of *creation* in English is not confined to the rather restrictive theological meaning of bringing into existence something out of nothing. By creation often we intend the product of human ingenuity or simply the adornment of some existing thing. The juxtaposition of wealth and creation is I believe a relatively new usage which has yet to settle to a universally accepted meaning. Wealth creation has about it a certain patina of respectability. It is an up-market term among economists, politicians and even theologians. It is aimed at a reality which does not include just vulgar riches or even involve sweat. It seems superior to the mind-dulling repetitive operations of our industrial past and eludes the accusations of being committed to Mammon, even though, sadly, both are still part of the human experience. With this in mind I shall explore briefly the roots of a Catholic view of *'Wealth Creation'*.

The Old Testament view of wealth is complex. It appears not to have been an issue for the Israelites in their earliest experience as a people. However once the Land was occupied and city dwelling established, various moral issues became the concern of the teachers and prophets. Both the blessing and dangers of wealth are stated. A difficult theological question for the Jews was the compounding of their convictions that wealth indicated God's blessing upon His favoured ones coupled with the reality that among the wealthy were sinners and those who were betraying the God-given ideals of the people.

Jesus Himself proposed a radically new approach to the problem. He resolved the dichotomy between wealth seen as God's blessing and the reality that the affluent were often clearly sinners. His solution was to remind His followers that all human affairs, including that of wealth creation and accumulation, had to be ordered in the light of the human being's ultimate destiny in God. Thus for Jesus all wealth has to be viewed in the context of the eschatological reality which each human being is to face. We will be judged at the end of our life on earth. One's eternal destiny will be determined by the quality of our duty to the Creator as expressed by the care and service exercised in respect of one's fellow human being. This is for Jesus the key to the use of wealth. Jesus offers no directions on work or wealth in themselves. He simply assumes these as part of the reality of human existence. It is the accumulation of wealth for its own sake and reliance upon wealth for happiness and fulfilment that He shows to be foolish and destructive of human dignity.

Time does not permit a review of the passages from the New Testament which support my assertions. I believe that a study both of the church Fathers and the medieval theologians show that this is the radical view of wealth accumulation which underpins the questions they raised, and sought to answer, over the consequences of the dangers to the human spirit which arise from riches and possessions. It is I believe by reason of *this focus upon the dangers to the human spirit which arise from riches*, that the theologians, teachers and writers of the Catholic Church had not used the term 'wealth creation' in their presentation of the gospel insights on possessions and riches. This may explain too why as far as I have been able to investigate, the term 'wealth creation' is not used as such in the teaching documents emanating from the Second Vatican Council or the Holy See.

In many ways 'wealth creation' is a term which states the obvious in Catholic thought applied to the human condition. The Catholic tradition (which is of course shared with many others) is that God created this universe and placed the human race in it as its crown and completion. This initial gift of lordship over creation is found in the Genesis narrative of creation. Only after the fall does this lordship become onerous or dangerous to the human hope of eternal happiness. Even so, the lordship of mankind over creation is not removed in punishment for sin. It is from the initial understanding of the human condition that Catholic social teaching on the human condition takes its starting point. That teaching develops by reflection upon the current reality of the human condition at the time the teaching is in formation.

It is important to recall that the span of the teaching from Pope Leo XIII in *Rerum Noverum*, 15-5-1891 to *Centesimus Annus*, 2-2-1991, of the present Pope, had as its backcloth a century of transition in many parts of the world from a rural society to one transformed by technology and the information technology revolution. It has been a hundred years of the most rapid and universal change in the material circumstances of the human condition that our race had ever experienced. Within this ever changing scene Catholic social teaching, including reflection on economic matters expressed by the Pope, Bishops and theologians of the church, has developed as new visions and possibilities for the human race appeared. However, some basic insights endure since these are founded in the revelation of God's will in Jesus Christ.

In the teaching of the Popes over the last century, the gift of the material creation of Adam and Eve is interpreted as much more than a simple gift to our first parents in which they were to enjoy an earthly paradise. The process shown in Genesis II, 18-20 of bringing the animals before Adam to name and the general license to use all things is to be understand as a gift to the whole human race. This gift is expressed in the phrase 'the universal destination of material goods'. This teaching appeared even prior to that of Leo XIII in *Rerum Novarum* and is continued in the teaching of subsequent Popes. John XXIII in *Mater et Magistra* (para. 119) states:

> Our predecessors have time and again insisted on the social function inherent in the right of private ownership, for its cannot be denied that in the plan of the Creator all of this world's goods are primarily intended for the support of the whole human race.

This approach has been greatly developed by the present Pope.

There is no doubt that wealth creation comes about through human work. Using the basic resources provided by the material creation itself, the human being not by chance but of intent applies the power of his intellect often coupled to the effort of his body, to shape the things of our world, giving them value to himself and to other human beings which they did not formerly have. The present Pope in the Encyclical Letter *Laborem Exercens* (para. 6), explores the notion of work, concluding that the primary measure of work is man himself who is the subject of work. This apparently innocuous principle has profound implications for the assignment of value to any work done or any systems of organisation of the work itself or of the political arrangements regulating the society of which the worker is a member.

In his most recent Encyclical Letter *Centesimus Annus*, Pope John Paul devotes a whole chapter to the exploration of private property and the universal destination of material goods. It is the combination of this notion with the acceptance that man is the measure of work, by which wealth is created, that constitutes the foundation of a specific and developing body of teaching in the modern Catholic tradition which is applicable to 'wealth creation'. This teaching first developed at a time when the human race was perceived as apparently permanently divided, and so isolated, in distinct and often hostile nation states, competing for the apparently unlimited material resources available. This perception has altered radically. It has been replaced by a unitary vision of the human race inhabiting a planet of very finite resources. It is this reality expressed as a vision of 'one world' which has a major influence on modern Catholic social teaching.

For many centuries the church has asserted that it is legitimate to exercise private ownership of some material goods. This conviction derives from a number of sources. Undoubtedly the commands of the decalogue prohibiting theft and covetousness imply private ownership. Thus one human has rights over material things which are to be respected by all others. This set the scene for the development of the Christian tradition through many centuries respecting private or individual ownership. In the face of a number of social and political factors, for example the feudal system, and the nineteenth century developments of theories and practice of total common ownership by the state of all material goods, the church felt obliged to insist upon the essential need and advantage conveyed to human dignity and fulfilment by some personal and exclusive ownership of material goods. However, this right has never been elevated to an absolute.

Pope John Paul reminds us that:

> God gave the earth to the whole human race for the sustenance of all its members, without excluding or favouring anyone. This is *the foundation of the universal destination of the earth's goods*... But the earth does not yield its fruits without a particular human response to God's gift, that is to say, without work. It is through work that man, using his intelligence and exercising his freedom, succeeds in dominating the earth and making it a fitting home. In this way, he makes part of the earth his own, precisely the part he has acquired through work; this is the *origin of individual property*. Obviously, he also has the responsibility not to hinder others from having their own part of God's gift; indeed he must cooperate with others so that together all can dominate the earth.[1]

After this brief review of 'wealth creation' and its relationship to private ownership as it appears in Catholic teaching, I turn to a consideration of 'competition' as seen in the light of the values of the Christian gospel. I do this following the suggestion of Pope

John Paul II in the Encyclical Letter *Sollicitudo Rei Socialis* issued by Pope John Paul on the 30-12-1987 to mark twenty years from the publication by Pope Paul VI of his Encyclical Letter *Populorum Progressio* on human economic development. Pope John Paul suggests that the evils of injustice and deprivation of many in the world today should be subjected to the analysis and directives for action found in the Church's social teaching. The Pope insists that the Church's social doctrine is not a third way between liberal capitalism and Marxist collectivism, nor even a possible alternative to other solutions less radically opposed to one another. It constitutes a category of its own. It is not an ideology but rather seeks to be an accurate formulation of the results of careful reflection on the complex realities of human existence and the international order in the light of faith and the Church's tradition. (SRS para. 41). Some of the positions adopted by the Pope are useful starting points for our consideration of 'competition'.

The Pope acknowledges that the experience of the present time seems to indicate that on the level of individual nations and international relations, *the free market* is the most efficient instrument for utilizing resources and effectively responding to needs. He also notes that the free market has its limitations so that prior to the logic of a fair exchange of goods and the forms of justice appropriate to it, there exists something which is due to man because he is man, by reason of his lofty dignity. That something must include the possibility of survival and of making a contribution to the common good of humanity (CA 34). This establishes a priority which must illuminate and if necessary restrict the notion of the free market applied within a specific economy. Thus it seems that an individual economy must be built upon a society of free work, of enterprise and of participation. Now these factors are to be encouraged to flourish and this must be the business for all including the organs of political and social duty. Neither the State nor Capital should be so in control that absolute dominance is exercised over the citizen to the damage of the free and personal nature of human work.

The Pope acknowledges that legitimate role of profit as an indication that a business is functioning well.[2] From the fact of making a profit one can deduce that productive resources have been property used and human needs satisfied. But he insists that profitability is not the only indicator of a firm's condition. It is possible for the accounting side of the business to be in order, yet the work force which is the firm's most valuable asset might have been humiliated and their dignity offended. This is both morally wrong and fraught with adverse consequences for the firm's economic efficiency and future. Indeed the prospects for its existence in the long-term must be regarded as very precarious.

These considerations lay a foundation for some specific comment upon competition. 'Competition' describes a complex reality in the human experience. It is associated with a great variety of human activities such as sport, human relationships, business and economics, politics etc. Essential to the notion of 'competition' is the element of striving to achieve. From this follows the consequence of out-performing any other or others who are engaged in the same pursuit. The motives of anyone engaged in competition can be varied. In one case the individual is motivated by a general desire to excel or achieve without any or much reference to the others involved. In other cases it may be that the desire simply to come first and so put down or behind one the others, is central to the competitor. In some cases 'competition' is seen as contest not with other human beings but other forces such as nature.

Since 'competition' is an element in a great variety of human activities we must be alert to the need to delineate as exactly as we can what we mean by it when referring to a particular activity under our review. Michael Novak in his *The Spirit of Democratic Capitalism*, sees competition as one of six theological doctrines used to establish a Theology of democratic capitalism. Competition appears as the third doctrine which includes the Trinity; the Incarnation; competition; original sin; the separation of realms; caritas. Novak explores in detail each of his 'doctrines'. With regard to competition he concludes his exploration by asserting:

..it seems wrong to conclude that the spirit of competition is foreign to the gospels, and that in particular, the competition for money is mankind's most moral spiritual danger.[3]

Some license in the use of terms must be allowed for so a creative a writer as Novak. While competition is rightly viewed as a human reality I am not able to agree that it is right to so readily describe it as a 'theological doctrine' even taking this term very loosely. Neither am I at ease with Novak's exploration of the theological consequences or significance of competition. Some further reflection is needed. I shall try, however inadequately, to do this.

As far as I can discover there is no place in the Gospels where Jesus is shown as castigating competition as such. This is consistent with His general attitude to conditions in the world into which He came. One is struck by His attitude of realism in His selection of materials for His teaching in parables: the king debating whether he had the forces to oppose another king (LK XIV, 31 *et seq.*) the smart-alec steward providing for himself when caught out and facing unemployment (LK XVI, 1-7); the judge who acts under pressure of demand and importunity rather than that of justice (LK XVIII, 1-5) etc. This realism is extended to His appreciation of His own mission as not being one of an arbiter on the material problems which He met in His own Palestinian experience (LK XII, 13 *et seq.*).

We must not conclude that Jesus was opposed to or simply withdrawn from the affairs of the world into which He came. The greater part of His life was lived as an artisan in Nazareth. He keenly observed the physical circumstances of everyday life, as may be seen by the accuracy of the details which He constructed His parables and illuminated His teaching. But He insisted that for Himself personally His mission was to establish a recognition of the supremacy of His Father's will for the human race. That will required observance of a fundamental law: love of God above all else, to which must be coupled love of neighbour. Jesus saw and taught clearly how the second percept of love is at risk in human affairs when one human being seeks to dominate another. Jesus requires that such domination be not found among His followers (MK X, 42-45).

Jesus did not attack the system of ownership and property obtaining in Palestine in His times. His teaching 'implies neither sanction or condemnation of economic or class differences; all that Jesus' wholly religious outlook completely excludes, by making love the supreme law, is mutual scorn and enmity, exploitation from above and hatred from below'.[4] From this point of departure the Church was later able to draw concrete conclusions regarding the economic and social order. Such conclusions made it impossible for certain social institutions to persevere e.g. emperor worship, slavery etc. Jesus did not set out to construct a system of vocational morality. Yet His teaching is often sharpest against those who are rich e.g. LK, VI, 24. However, this teaching is not directed at riches in themselves but at the thirst for power and forgetfulness of God which their possession induces.

From these very general observations on the teaching of Jesus Christ we move to consider the reality of 'competition' in human economic affairs in the light of the Catholic tradition. As far as I can find, there is no modern specific teaching by the pastors of the Roman Church on the notion of competition. There is a substantial body of traditional teaching, largely of the casuistic style, on contracts, general trading and charging interest etc. This teaching is concerned with giving guidelines for individual consciences on moral problems which can arise in the course of commercial activity. Precise directions on commercial transactions are derived from a number of principles: the duty to fulfil contracts which are based in justice; the need always to observe certain priorities in meeting human needs; the requirement of acting to serve the common good of the society of which one is part etc. Yet this teaching is also rooted in the human reality. One of its favourite aphorisms in the sections on contracts is *caveat emptor*. Such a saying does not excuse deception but acknowledges the need of human diligence against deceit in commercial transactions.

Jesus Christ gave many warnings about the dangers of wealth and of over-focusing on the world's goods. The general reason for these warnings is to be found in the Lord's concern that human beings can lose sight of the Creator in pursuing the goods of His creation. From this stance of the Lord I am reinforced in my conviction that there is no specific condemnation of competition as such to be found in Christ's teaching. However, where competition involves the search for dominion over another human being or the exclusion of any individual's duty to promote the common good, then violence is done to the values of the Christian gospel. I agree with Novak's premise that God is not committed to equality of treatment of each human being. But this does not contradict the essentially gratuitous and loving offer by God to all human beings of eternal salvation through Jesus Christ. The route to acceptance of this offer is found in service of God in and through our fellow human being. The question is thus posed for all commercial, economic and political transactions as to how that service is advanced or obstructed by competition.

To complement these considerations it seems to me necessary to assert that the enthronement of 'competition' as an absolute in human affairs, whether economic or political, is dangerous to the common good and the proper fulfilment of each human being as a child of God. This is so because to place 'competition' as an absolute in human affairs puts at risk other and prior human realities such as individual dignity, and the essentially social dimension of human existence. Thus, when the term 'competition' is used in respect of social, political and economic affairs, then the reality of what is meant by the term must be taken into account in judging the ethical status of the action proposed or the stance adopted.

Although I can find no specific reference in the formal teaching of the pastors of the Catholic Church on competition, there is an illuminating reference in *Octogesima Anno,* to the need to avoid that type of liberal ideology which exalts individual freedom:

by withdrawing it from every limitation, by stimulating through exclusive seeking of interest and power, and by considering social solidarities as more or less automatic consequences of individual initiatives, not as an aim and a major criterion of the value of social organisations'.[5]

It is wrong, in the view of Pope John Paul II, expressed in his address to the Mexican business community at Durango in 1990, to claim that the social teaching of the church flatly condemns an economic theory. Rather the Pope insists that the church wishes to encourage critical reflection on social processes. An economic or political theory or process which puts in jeopardy or violates the dignity of the human person must be rejected. However, it is for the experts in society to continue the search for valid and lasting solutions for human needs that do not deflect from human nature which is made in the image and likeness of God. Competition is an important factor to be taken into account in this regard.

Recently Peter Morgan, Director General of the Institute of Directors' has embarked upon the composition of the credo for directors of companies. I must commend the intention of the Director in composing such a Credo for Directors. Much of what he writes makes a strong even essential demand for the search for truth and the good in discharging one's duty as a director of a company. The Credo contains then a welcome reminder of the ethical dimension in this very important role in modern society. The issue of the Credo offers a useful example of how in practice the reality of competition poses questions which are a challenge to human dignity.

Item one of the Credo has as its first point: 'A belief in free market capitalism and competition'. This is a rather absolutist statement. The question must be asked: what is the effect of this statement on directors? Does it put at risk their dedication to the ethical dimension of their roles as directors of companies? Because of this possibility it is important for directors to be reminded on a regular basis that the company whose affairs they direct has to be seen not only in the context of its own internal dynamic of operation and success but also in the reality of the wider human society of which it is an important part. In addition directors must accept that there are basic human rights which may not be deliberately and directly impugned as a result of the operations of their company. It is in the light of these principles that competition as presented in the Credo and its explanatory parts has to be evaluated with respect to its consequence for ethical issues.

It seems to me that Directors are safe in rejecting opinions which hold that any form of competition is essentially opposed to the Christian Gospel. This I have tried to demonstrate in preceding paragraphs. The Credo's view of competition is expanded in the statement 'we mean competition not cartels'. A cartel, understood as a union of manufacturers or traders to control production, marketing arrangements, prices, etc., has notoriously been associated with the attempt to gain and hold power over others. This is often seen as being without regard for fairness and with the intent of denying to others the prospect of exercising their own skills and insights. Such action is clearly wrong. Thus the contrasting of competition and cartels in the Code must be right.

It is further stated in the explanation of the Code 'We know competition means winners and losers and we accept that. We believe that living with market forces makes the economy stronger'. The Code then goes on to state its stance with respect to Government intervention in business (which it rejects) yet affirms the duty of Government to establish an appropriate legislative and regulatory environment, together with sound money. It is also states that a company must accept responsibility for promoting the common good.

The juxtaposition of 'competition' and 'winners and losers' occasions immediate sensitivity among those who have regard for their fellow human beings. On the one hand, it seems that attempts by state intervention to eliminate 'competition' have resulted in profoundly inefficient economies quite incapable of supplying an adequate level of life for the citizens. On the other hand, 'winners and losers' gives an image of haves and have-nots caught in a cycle of abundance and power for some, with destitution and, power-lessness for others.

The teaching of Pope John Paul II in Chapter IV of *Centesimus Annus*, 14-5-1991, to which I have already directed your attention (para. 10), gives a basis for an approach which is necessary for the reversal of the inhuman effects deriving from the 'winners and losers' factor in a free market economy. This chapter is entitled 'Private property and the universal destination of material goods'. In this phrase is gathered the teaching of the Catholic Church in the last century, of the right to private property coupled with the gift by God to the whole human race of this earth for the sustenance of all its members, without excluding or favouring anyone. From this point of departure the Pope develops his teaching on man being the measure of work; that work is with others and for others; man's principle resource in shaping this world is man himself.

I have referred above to the Pope's statement: 'It would appear that, on the level of individual nations and of international relations, *the free market* is the most efficient instrument for utilizing resources and effectively responding to needs'. Yet the Pope warns of the limitations of this approach saying:

> But there are many human needs which find no place on the market. It is a strict duty of justice and truth not to allow fundamental human needs to remain unsatisfied for even prior to the logic of the fair exchange of goods and the forms of justice appropriate to it, there exists *something which is due to man because he is man* by reason of his lofty dignity'.[6]

Continuing this line of thought, the Pope excludes the absolute predominance of capital, the possession of the means of production and of the land, in contrast to the free and personal nature of human work:

> What is proposed as an alternative is not the socialist system, which in fact turns out to be state capitalism but rather a society of free work, of enterprise and of participation. Such a society is not directed against the market, but demands that the market be appropriately controlled by the

forces of society and by the state, so as to guarantee that the basic needs of the whole of society are satisfied'.[7]

Pope John Paul acknowledges the legitimate role of profit as an indication that a business is functioning well. But profit is not to be taken as the only indicator of a firm's condition. A business is a community of persons who in various ways are endeavouring to satisfy their basic needs, and who form a participating group at the service of the whole of society. Finally the Pope insists, with particular reference to the international scene, that capitalism should not be seen as the only model of economic organisation.[8]

By examining part of the Credo for the Institute of Directors on 'competition' I have tried to explore what are the theological applications of this factor. It may be that the 'losers and gainers' approach is to be seen as a restricted view of the matter. It may be that a better phrase to describe 'competition' in human commercial and economic activity is 'free work, enterprise and participation'. In this way, what is put aside is the notion of assault or attack upon other human beings. Yet at the same time there is preserved the reality that 'competition' is an inevitable consequence of the human condition since we humans are not in complete control of ourselves or our world. The search for doing things in a better way; the constant inventive capacity of the human spirit; the fulfilment of the Genesis command to occupy and use this earth indicate that the human race is destined by God's gift to man. Rather than describing this dynamic reality as 'competition' it is best summarised in phrase of 'enterprise and participation'.

A factor which must always be kept in mind in considering matters which touch upon the fundamentals of the human condition is that of sin. It is Catholic teaching that Christ has overcome the disaster of sin in our first parents and in each member of the human race, yet all (except Christ and the Blessed Virgin) are touched by sin. The consequences of overweening self-love and thereby exclusion of God and our neighbour which is at the heart of sin, are manifest in our world. Hence the need for laws and codes which remind us of our dignity and that of others. Competition, then, can offer the opportunity for sin or service of others. While sin is always rooted in personal choice to offend God, nonetheless this aberration in the human experience can be taken into the structures of society and become part of economic and social systems. Thus 'competition' from which these things flow must be subjected to the spirit of the Gospel and so transformed into an opportunity for service.

It seems that there is no escaping the conviction that competition is an essential ingredient for the successful functioning of modern economic systems. Indeed, it is no doubt held by some that it is necessary for a successful world wide system of economic and political progress. At this level there are many voices which raise doubts on such a principles. These doubts turn for evidence to the ecological problems which are currently confronting a number of countries and are said to threaten the world environment to the extent that the future of the human species is at risk. To the unbridled consequences of untrammelled competition Pope John Paul in the letter *Solicitudo Rei Socialis* presents the need for 'solidarity'. This term indicates the universal brotherhood of mankind under God by which the individuals and communities who are in need must be the active concern of all human beings. This concern in especially urgent and pressing upon those individuals and communities who have an abundance of the goods of this earth.

Solidarity then is the practical application of the principle enshrined in the title of the fourth chapter of *Centesimus Annus*: 'Private property and the universal destination of material goods' to which reference has been made earlier in this paper. Unless the gospel values, which are proclaimed by the Catholic Church in union with many other human beings of goods will, are applied to wealth creation and the political and economic systems which are associated with this essential human activity, then human beings, human communities and the human race itself are at risk to dangers which not only would destroy human dignity but also human existence on this planet.

Notes

1   Pope John Paul II, *Centesimus Annus*, para. 31.

2   *Centesimus Annus*, para. 35.

3   Novak, Michael, *The Spirit of Democratic Capitalism*, (2nd edition), London: IEA Health and Welfare Unit, 1991, pp. 344-349.

4   Schnackenburg, R., *Moral Teaching of the New Testament*, p. 123.

5   Pope Paul VI, *Octogesima Anno*, 14-5-1971, N.26.

6   *Centesimus Annus*, para. 34.

7   *Centesimus Annus*, para. 35.

8   *Centesimus Annus*, para. 35.

Novak, Tawney and Moral Freedom

Simon Robinson

Introduction

This paper is written in response to a challenge from Michael Novak in a recent seminar held at the Institute of Economic Affairs.[1] The challenge was to social democrats and thinkers such as Novak to enter into greater dialogue.

To cut through the problems inherent in defining different 'positions' I intend to contribute to the dialogue by comparing Novak's thoughts with one particular writer on social democracy. At first sight the choice of R H Tawney might seem an unlikely one, not least because the only references that Novak has to him shows him as antithetical to capitalism.[2] However, whilst Tawney was very much against some forms of capitalism he was not against all. He recognized that there were different kinds and that capitalism had had the effect of encouraging important virtues.[3] Equally, whilst Tawney was an advocate of nationalisation this was no doctrinaire advocacy. For Tawney, nationalisation was to be selective, and for particular purposes, i.e. to improve efficiency, democracy and community.

Tawney was a liberal egalitarian and as such was concerned for the virtues of individual responsibility and self-reliance as much as for distributional patterns which enable individuals to develop. This was in the context of the primary principle of equality of respect, a principle which generated the twin principles of freedom and fellowship. He was also a Christian and as such he was aware of and used concepts such as sin.

These principles appear very close to the four headings that Novak sees as basic to the Jewish, Christian, and humanistic vision; human fallibility and sin; creativity; community; and freedom.[4]

Given these striking similarities between Novak and Tawney, similarities which are much closer than those between Walzer and Novak, I will focus the area of debate upon principles and in particular on the principle of liberty.[5]

Liberty

Both Novak and Tawney lay claim to a view of liberty which does not fit easily into Berlin's distinction between negative and positive liberty.[6] Both see importance in the defence of rights, through negative political liberty. Both also move beyond the idea of positive liberty which Berlin characterizes as freedom to develop capacities. Berlin argues that such a liberty clashes with negative liberty precisely because it requires that such capacities be equalized, something that would require coercion. Instead both Tawney and Novak move to claim the middle ground of moral freedom. This is a freedom which is appropriated freely by individuals, and therefore does not necessarily clash with the defence of rights. It is also a freedom to do one's duty, in Acton's words 'to do what one ought', and this is contrasted strongly with freedom as license.[7] Tawney argues strongly for liberty as being contextual. There is not one liberty but many, and their acceptance depends upon the purpose of the liberty. The highest purpose is to serve and through this do one's duty. Like Novak, Tawney does not attempt to prescribe the exact content of that duty. This is precisely for the individuals to work out in their own context.

Given this, it is not surprising that both Novak and Tawney see such freedom as located in the action of reflective decision making. This is characterised by Novak in terms of the individual taking responsibility for decisions, and thus achieving genuine control or power. For Tawney such responsibility and control are also crucial elements of a liberty which involves 'the opportunity for self-direction'.[8] For both writers there is also a concern for independence of thought and action, and an abhorrence of dependency and subservience.

This freedom involves the identification, development and 'habituation of quite considerable moral skills', which for Novak include temperance, just judgement and practical wisdom. The development of such skills, so that they become second nature, requires 'painstaking discipline'.[9] Tawney too sees the importance of developing necessary virtues and skills, including self reliance, self respect, mutual confidence and enterprise.[10]

For Novak this is a freedom which is at the root of human autonomy, responsibility and dignity, 'and that enables the creature to act in the image of the Creator'.[11] Tawney does not use such creationist images explicitly, preferring to focus on the Incarnation. However, he argues for the participation of humans in meaningful work and relationships, which includes participation in responsibility and decision-making in work.

Novak sees the responsibility for the development of this moral freedom as at least initially in the hands of the individual. This effort is characterised as a response to a vocation, and also as individuals conquering and appropriating such freedom for themselves. This does not deny the responsibility of society to enable such freedom. On the contrary, society must develop the kind of culture which can enable the practice of such freedom. Society must

> constantly invent institutions able to expand and, as it were, to allow air and space for the flowering of this liberty amongst their citizens.[12]

It is striking that Tawney too saw the importance of the individual accepting the responsibility for the development of such freedom, locating the seat of power in the soul. Equally striking is the way that Tawney looks to the development of intermediate institutions which will enable such power to be developed. In education and industry he looked to the development of a culture which would encourage 'activity, free initiative, and the power of self-direction'.[13]

At the base of this is a concern for the creative and responsive individual whose unique needs will not be met by the bland uniformity of absolute equality. Thus different needs would not be met in the same way, 'but by devoting equal care to ensuring that they are met in the different ways most appropriate to them'.[14] Tawney, so famous for equality, has as his base a person-regarding equality rather than simply a desire to equalise resources for all. In all this he advocates democratic experiments in intermediate groups, with the end of being able to achieve the appropriate response to the needs of the group members and beyond.

All of this points to a distinctive, middle view of freedom which both Tawney and Novak are claiming. It indicates far greater similarity than might be expected and at the least provides that basis from which the kind of discussion that Novak advocates can be carried out. To do this more thoroughly I intend to examine moral freedom under two heads: the concept and its relation to other important principles; and the constraints on moral freedom, both in terms of sin and of the constraints that may be necessary to enable such a freedom to flourish.

The Concept of Moral Freedom

Firstly, Novak's view of moral liberty is very much Thomist, with its stress on ordering the passions and gaining self-mastery. This is about the individual developing autonomy through reflective, deliberative decision-making. Freedom is precisely gained through the acquisition of the skills and qualities which underlie these activities. This 'ordered liberty' requires 'for its exercise a degree of manly or womanly strength (*virtus*) sufficient to achieve internal self-mastery of one's passions and appetites, so as to judge matters as coolly, realistically and dispassionately as reflection and deliberate choice require'.[15] The stress, and so the moral content of this liberty, is upon the individual and enabling the individual to be a more effective decision maker. There is no stress upon the moral claims of others and thus no sense of the decision maker responding to such claims. In all this he actually appears more concerned with what is a negative and individualist form of moral freedom i.e. to ensure that conscience is protected and that individuals each take full responsibility for their decisions.[16]

Secondly, Novak's justification for his view of moral liberty is both individualist and consequentialist. The individualist argument is linked into the view of individuals as acting in the image of the Creator. It is precisely moral freedom which lies at the 'root of human autonomy, responsibility and dignity' all of which enable the individual to act in God's image.[17] This moral freedom, then, is necessary for a person to act in God's image, and it arises from specific 'internally derived constraints and standards'.

The consequentialist justification of moral liberty is precisely that of the moral invisible hand. It is not just that the exercise of moral liberty would lead to better distribution of resources, it is also that it would lead to cooperation, i.e. to a positive moral end. There is, writes Novak, a built-in drive 'towards mutually agreeable exchange', quite simply because one person's economic purposes can only be secured by voluntary cooperation with many others in rule-based, reasoned activities'.[18]

Novak's view of morality here seems to be identified with the practical decision making that he extols. Perhaps the crucial point about this morality is that it is determined by the individual, ensuring no moral coercion. Finally, Novak argues that such freedom is at the base of genuine community. He compares this to forms of community which are exclusive and where the idea of solidarity is coercive. A more acceptable view of community is precisely one in which reflection and choice amongst its members are enabled. Such intermediate communities are essential then to the development of moral liberty, and at the same time depend upon it. Novak sees a healthy capitalism as the basis for the development of such communities, for 'markets have a centripetal force; their inner dynamic aims at mutual, civil, reasoned agreements'.[19]

For Novak this provides the exciting prospect of a distinctive form of community, crucially based upon the free decision of individuals to enter it, and form an appropriate contract.

In turning to Tawney we see a more complex and broader view of moral liberty. Like Novak he is concerned for control, including control of the passions. Indeed, he argues that the supreme evil of industrial society is not poverty but rather the absence of liberty 'i.e. of the opportunity of self direction'.[20] However, this liberty has a social, and an economic as well as a moral strand. Freedom is a social concept precisely because any individual's freedom can affect another's, thus 'freedom for the strong is oppression for the poor'.[21] Here freedom is directly related to power and the power to control one's life in significant areas. Such power, Tawney argues, is both a function of the individual's personality—'the seat of power is in the soul'—but also of material resources. He does not form a necessary link between poverty and lack of freedom. He does argue, however, that lack of control of material resources can radically affect not only the control of individual's situation but specifically the moral freedom which the individual wishes to develop. This can be so in various ways.

Firstly, without some basic economic control the individual can easily lose the will to move away from systems of dependency. Secondly, the very relationships that one is a part of can have the effect of diminishing moral freedom. Certain economic relationships, in particular those which treat the individual as a means and not an end, tend to encourage subservience and dependence, and this involves a complete loss of liberty. Thirdly, lack of material resources can lead to the individual being unable to fulfil moral obligations. In effect Tawney talks about the denial of choice in terms of moral freedom. Real empowering of individuals therefore involves enabling them to fulfil their duty—to the self, in terms of personal development, and to others, both in terms of basic obligation of respect owed to all, and in terms of the duty involved in particular relationships, from family through to community.

Such relationships are not simply contractual but part of the network of moral relationships in which man finds himself. Hence Tawney can refer to duties to the community which the individual 'does not choose, and responsibilities created for him'.[22] As noted, the precise content of such duties is not prescribed by Tawney, but rather left to the individual. In Tawney then the stress in moral freedom is the freedom to do ones duty, and thus upon the responsibility of individuals not just for themselves but also for others in the context of their network of moral relationships. Control, self direction, and effective decision making are seen very much in terms of being enabled to serve in this way. This demands that reflection upon duty be a central part of any decision making, and that the individual be enabled socially and economically to fulfil his or her duties.

The differences with Novak are confirmed once one examines Tawney's justification of freedom to serve. Firstly, he uses a personalist argument, seeing this freedom as to do with the well-being of the individual, something which is tied in to the fulfilment of duty. He argues that, 'people want rights—freedom, in order that they can perform duties'. The performing of such duties is 'what spiritual well-being consists in', and through this the ideas of duty and freedom are reconciled.[23]

Secondly, however, he sees quite clearly a deontological base to this position which directly contradicts the consequentialism of Novak. Novak saw the good consequences of cooperation directly caused by the exercise of moral freedom and reflective decision making, such that the economic benefits of cooperation would become clear to all. Tawney certainly used consequentialist arguments for cooperation but ultimately cooperation and 'right relationships', in terms of the fulfilling obligations, form the moral ground of equality of respect on which he builds. Thus, 'even if the way of cooperation did not produce all the economic advantages expected from it, we should continue to use it'.[24]

A great deal of the comparison at this point comes down to different views of what morality is. As noted above, Novak tends to identify morality with practical wisdom and decision making. Tawney is equally convinced that there should be reflective decision making, but sees morality as to do first and foremost with unconditional equality of respect and thus sees decision making as firmly in the context of the basic principles of equality of respect, freedom and community, involving a response to the moral claims of all those who are involved in any situation.

Novak is rightly concerned that socialism should not take the concept of community to itself. For any 'position' or party to attempt to own particular concepts and principles is simplistic in the extreme. What is far more important is to determine how common words are interpreted and used differently. In that light it once again becomes apparent that Novak and Tawney have a great deal of overlap in the meaning of the term of community and its relation to freedom, but that differences emerge. Both see community as requiring free assent, and as being important to the development of freedom. Both see the importance of caring relationships in the enabling of the virtues necessary for moral freedom. Both also see the importance of developing the responsibility of the individual in community. What is once again not clear is that they aim to enable the same freedom. Novak is concerned for the development of the decision maker and thus of the skills of reflectivity. Tawney sees community as enabling individuals to serve and to fulfil their duties. It is thus that he strongly argues for participatory equality alongside distributive equality. Neither writer seems aware of the full complexities of community, with Tawney stressing the existing claims of community networks and Novak stressing the idea of community begun anew through free contract. Future dialogue would need to examine these positions further, for it could be argued that there is both the element of free negotiation (not least in defining roles) and of givenness, in any community, to some degree. What becomes more important, than claiming the correctness of different views of community is the need to develop means of negotiation in all communities, and to recognize moral claims where they do exist.

One absence of freedom is the state of dependency, and both examine this, especially in work related and community contexts. Novak's focus of dependency tends to be on those who are out of work. Hence he is concerned to develop responsibility amongst the unemployed.[25] Tawney focuses, as noted above, upon dependency at work, and in particular how oppressive relationships can lead to subservience. There is some truth in both points. It is perfectly possible that dependency can be encouraged in both contexts, and in the case of work not just through fear. Both writers, however, fall in to the trap of falsely characterising the major groups both in and out of work. For Tawney the ordinary worker tended to be a very moral individual who was concerned in the first place to do his or her duty. He was not always alive to the possibility that the average man was not necessarily inclined to the development of moral freedom. From Novak there is the equally remarkable view of the business person who through the application of practical wisdom almost naturally makes good decisions which lead to cooperation.

Empirical evidence suggests a far more complex picture. There are good examples of cooperation.[26] There are equally good examples of the way in which a market which is not regulated can actually constrain companies from acting in a responsive manner. Thus, e.g. where there are no government regulations on the emission of waste, a company would be penalizing itself if it determined to move for costly effluent control. Taking extreme positions can easily take us away from dialogue altogether, and there are clearly signs of both writers trying to defend different set positions.

However, such signs of dogmatism take second place when actual situations are analysed in the light of the above debate. In the case of the unemployed and those in receipt of benefit, for instance, Novak wants to advocate that the unemployed should be encouraged to develop independence and responsibility. One suggested way of achieving this would be to offer some form of work in exchange for benefit.[27]

Such methods as this aim to diminish the growth of a dependency culture. In the light of the above debate this in itself would be unsatisfactory. Both Novak and Tawney are agreed that the movement to moral freedom occurs within, and is enabled by, community, as given flesh by intermediary groups. Far more important than the simple contract for the exchange of benefits then would be the context in which such an exchange took place. Such a community would require to negotiate a role with the beneficiary, affirming their place in the community and the worth of any contribution. Several things block such an approach at the present. The unemployed are excluded from the community of work, and often have either no community to relate to during the day or have communities which do not enable them to take responsibilities. Equally, because of the greater renumeration of paid work there is the implicit message that the contribution of anyone who simply receives benefit is not as important or worthy as the contribution of someone who is in work. It is not the place of this paper to examine such issues in detail. However, they do underline the danger of communities where the individual is only valued for the contribution that he or she makes and only rewarded for the practice of skills in particular contexts. This also confirms a basic difference between Novak and Tawney. Novak looks primarily to the taking of moral freedom, with the implication that this will be rewarded. For Tawney freedom to serve is in the context of a community which first and foremost values others unconditionally and looks to develop self-reliance through that.

Another important area that might be examined in taking this dialogue further is that of business decision making. Empirical evidence does not suggest that Novak's moral freedom naturally leads to community and cooperation in this field. On the contrary, examples such as the Nestlé baby milk controversy point to a lack of cooperation and trust.[28] The underlying cause of that controversy was precisely a lack of reflection on the responsibilities of all those who had some stake in the issue. Such reflection would have revealed responsibilities at several levels amongst the stakeholders. Some of these were related to simple contracts, others were not. Some responsibilities were not well defined, e.g. with Nestlé assuming that they had the responsibility of education in the use of dried baby milk. Other stakeholder responsibilities, such as those of the local health services and authorities were hardly developed at all. The disastrous consequences of the Nestlé case would indicate that any reflection and decision making demands the consideration of mutual responsibility of all the stakeholders, and of ways in which they might be fulfilled. It would further indicate, along with Tawney, that creativity and decision making is not in essence an individualistic activity but one actually depending upon community reflection and a search for moral meaning and purpose in any given situation. Where Tawney fell short was in not giving further detail of how such an aim might be achieved.

What emerges at this stage is the conclusion that there is not one middle view of moral freedom but two. There are overlaps in meaning but both clearly have a very different stress which includes a different relationship between moral freedom and community, a different view of morality, different justifications and something of a tendency to try to defend different sectional interests. Moving beyond sectional interests it was suggested that a crucial further stage in the dialogue was to examine the different views of moral freedom in relation to particular contexts.

Constraints

Novak's concept of moral liberty paints a very positive picture of the market and the benefits of reasoned decision making. All liberty is nonetheless subject to the limitations of human sinfulness. Novak defines sin in this context as *'aversio a Deo*, that is a freely chosen course of separation from God, from reason, from cooperation with others, and from respect for the dignity of others'.[29]

The existence of sin requires that all social power must be 'divided, checked and hemmed around with auxiliary precautions.' Central to such control for Novak is the view of the three major 'power systems', the spheres of the economic, the political and the moral-cultural. He argues that the elites of all these spheres are not to be trusted and that 'the overwhelming persistence of human fallibility and sinfulness will counsel the effective separation of all three major systems of power into mutually independent hands'.[30] Despite his emphasis on the communitarian individual then,

Novak's description of sin tends to be both straightforwardly individualist and intentional. We are to see the act of sin as a freely chosen decision to move away from God and all the important principles that Novak sets down.

This is clearly an important concept of sin, and one which Tawney recognizes. However, Tawney explores quite another area of sin and fallibility, which is to do with group organization. In the light of an interactionist sociology he looks to how organisations can both lead to irresponsible behaviour but also enable good behaviour. This does not take away from the responsibility of the individual. Nor does Tawney see the answer to all problems as being in organization. However, oppressive organization can contribute to individuals losing the will to do their duty. This may be partly due to attitudes expressed through the organization, or simple lack of opportunity for people to serve and contribute in a meaningful way. It may also be to do with the ethos and expressed aim of the organization. Such effects may even occur with leaders who are perfectly well intentioned. Any decisions or structure that is determined upon is ultimately the expressions of the principles which underlie that decision or structure. A leader or manager may have the best of intentions and may well use all the skills of practical decision-making, and yet if the level of principles are not addressed and not related to practice it is possible for the decision or structure to reflect something quite other than was intended. The capitalism of Tawney's time reflected, in his judgement, a series of negative principles. These began with the denial of responsibility, the argument that an owner or executive is not responsible for the results of a course of action pursued in business. The second principle was the denial of personality, such that the 'mass of mankind' was treated as tools.

Finally came the denial of other than individual morality, and the denial of freedom.[31] Tawney was judging these principles from the evidence that he saw of the behaviour and organization of capitalism then. The broader point that emerges from Tawney's position for today is that without this level of moral reflection any company could be organised in ways quite contrary to the basic principles and intentions of the owners and executives, leading both to an ethos where moral responsibility is not encouraged, and possibly either disastrous consequences or immoral actions.

A good example is the organisation of large modern companies, where the structure of cost centres, each with the prime aim of achieving financial goals, can easily obscure the aims of any general or moral purpose clause in a company's mission statement. Other too frequent examples have led to disaster. The Sheen report on the sinking of the Herald of Free Enterprise clearly notes that there was a failure on two levels. Firstly, the prime purpose of the crew of the ferry was perceived by all the crew as to turn it round as quickly as possible in order to maximise the numbers of runs. Secondly, despite a clear code of practice the crew, who were directly involved in the disaster, did not feel any sense of responsibility for closing the bow doors. Individuals seemed to feel that they need not go beyond their role as set down in the code, and thus did not recognize a more general sense of responsibility, or sense of service beyond what was laid down for them in their contract.[32]

Sin in this situation is not a simple task of deciding to act against God but arises out of the organization and ethos of the corporation and the way in which relationships are handled. Fallible acts can occur literally without awareness. All of this points to the need to have safeguards against the irresponsible use of power, but also the need to develop an ethos for any corporation which will increase moral and social awareness and enable the business as a whole to be responsive and responsible. In addition to checks and codes this also requires the development of moral decision making skills and qualities amongst the staff.[33]

There are four ways that all this can be achieved: the development of government regulation so that companies are not penalised for seeking to enable moral freedom and to be responsive to the claims of stakeholders; the development of codes of professional and business ethics; the development of the organisation of business, with individuals being given greater freedom and responsibility through democracy; and the development of the skills, personal qualities, and social and moral awareness of the members of staff.[34] All in some form have been advocated by Tawney. He argued that the use of any one of these methods would not be effective by itself. In addition to changes in organization there needed to be the development of a 'social philosophy', something that could be perceived to be at the base of common purposes. Such shared purposes would of themselves be enabling, both providing a focus around which the cooperation could be developed, and also providing trust at the level of principle. This would be most effective if worked out by the members of the organization themselves, such a process enhancing commitment to those purposes. It would involve the discovery and affirmation of moral meaning, something Tawney thought could only occur in community, and essential to the development of community. All this would not therefore involve moral coercion.

As noted above Novak sees the division of social powers as necessary to counter human sinfulness. In one sense this is very important, in that if those in political power were to dictate moral thinking and economic treatment this would be totally coercive. Tawney, however, argues that morality is a part of all the other so-called spheres. Politics and economics are about the organization of aspects of society and government and are ultimately to be judged in moral terms, either in terms of consequences or of the moral rightness of the approach. Hence Tawney is concerned less with the division of powers and more with ways in which those issues of morality can be addressed in every human situation. For Tawney this meant rather a distribution of power. As noted above this was partly to do with giving greater freedom and responsibility to individuals. It was also about ensuring against concentrations of power in whatever form. Tawney is part of a long Christian Tradition which emphasises that concentrations of power and wealth tend to lead to irresponsible and sinful behaviour.[35] It is precisely this distribution of power through democracy that Tawney sees as the most effective way of guarding against totalitarianism.[36] This distribution of power involved a whole series of relationships which would make companies, for instance, more accountable. Accountability was to the workforce, to the professional bodies, which Tawney argued should strengthen their ethical codes, and to the public as a whole. Tawney believed that public opinion had great force and that the business of companies should be open to what he refers to as 'complete publicity'.[37]

Novak and Tawney then reveal different perspectives on sin and human fallibility. Starting from a social interactionist model, Tawney sees the checks and balances against sin as part of an integrated approach which also looks to the development of an intermediate group ethos which can in turn encourage the development of moral meaning and thus of moral freedom. Indeed the crucial strategy of distributing powers through democracy, participatory equality, is both a guard against the concentration of powers and an enabling of moral freedom, in the sense of freedom to serve. For Novak the question would perhaps be, how far can the combination or regulation and the distribution of power be achieved without coercion. Thus he prefers to view the question of sin, as with moral freedom, in a more individualist way.

Conclusion

The view of moral freedom which Michael Novak puts forward is very important, not least because of the way he ties this in to the importance of deliberate decision making, creativity and reflectivity. At the base of this is a vocational theology, with God calling the individual to be creative, to participate in work. In comparing it with the freedom to serve of Tawney's social democracy, it has become clear that despite clear overlaps in meaning there are in fact two distinct views of moral freedom. Novak stresses individual moral control, whilst Tawney stresses control in relation to fulfilling moral claims. Novak has an individualist justification and theology underlying his view of creativity, stressing God's call to the individual to participate in work, whereas Tawney sees a broader picture which involves mutual responsibility and a desire to enable others to fulfil that through freedom to serve. Tawney's underlying theology is more Incarnational, with God bestowing value on all persons, and values not arising from the labour of the individual. As a result whilst their approaches to the development of freedom and community seemed at first quite close, Tawney asks for much more in terms of an enabling framework from the government, from the companies and from all stakeholders. It is from this perspective that he looks to an increase in equality of opportunity, relative equality of resources, and perhaps above all relational equality. The latter is an equality of relationship discovered in community.

It must be said that there are times when the stance of both writers does not seem open to dialogue. Both are capable of scathing words delivered at socialism or capitalism. Both are capable of creating straw men. Having examined some of the similarities and differences it is clear that further dialogue has to move beyond that kind of false characterisation, or the selective use of empirical evidence, and I would suggest three areas in which this can be done in relation to moral freedom.

Firstly, the theology of creativity requires further analysis and development. Novak's view as stated ignores that social dimension of creativity, taking no account of the idea of the creative act in any situation as being the responsibility of all the stakeholders. Tawney's view requires more details of how such reflection and creation can be achieved in such a way as to avoid coercion.

Secondly, the whole area of decision making needs a more detailed and sophisticated analysis than either Novak or Tawney bring to bear. A good example of this is the underlying 'virtues' necessary for decision making. Nowhere do either of the writers begin to distinguish quite different elements involved, from personal qualities, through to attitudes, capacities and many different kinds of skills. Greater care in definition at this level would begin to clarify the precise needs of autonomy in decision making and thus what any community could begin to enable.[38]

Thirdly, there must be reflection on a wider range of policy and practice. Such reflection is necessary in order to determine what moral freedom might mean in practice. Moral freedom remains a general principle and the substantive content will vary according to different situations. Reflections on such situations will in turn affect how the general principle is viewed and take any debate to a much deeper level. Tawney himself accepted that whilst general principles might produce assent, their application will vary. All of this, however, requires the development of mechanisms for reflection, and of practical learning skills.

Only with developments such as these will any dialogue between social democracy and democratic capitalism begin to bear fruit, leading to greater openness and learning on both sides.

Notes

1 A Seminar given in the Institute of Economic Affairs on the 31 March 1992, on the subject of *Centesimus Annus*, and the Pope's view of the social assisted state.

2 See, for instance, Novak, M., *The Spirit of Democratic Capitalism*, (2nd edition), London: IEA,Health and Welfare Unite, 1991, p. 83.

3 *The Attack and Other Papers*, Allen and Unwin, 1953, p. 169 ff. See also *Commonplace Book*, Cambridge University Press, 1972 edn., (CB), p. 40.

4 Novak, M., *Morality, Capitalism and Democracy*, London: IEA Health and Welfare Unit, 1990, chapter 3.

5 *The Spirit of Democratic Capitalism*, p. 144.

6 Berlin, I., 'Two Concepts of Liberty', in *Political Philosophy*, A Quinton, (ed), Oxford, 1969, pp. 141-153.

7 *Morality, Capitalism and Democracy* p. 16.

8 CB p. 34.

9 *Morality, Capitalism and Democracy*, p. 17.

10 CB, p. 40-41.

11 *Morality, Capitalism and Democracy*, p. 18.

12 *Ibid.*, p. 19.

13 *Education: The Socialist Policy* (ESP), Tawney, R.H., principle author, *Independent Labour Party*, 1924. See also *The Radical Tradition*, Allen and Unwin, 1964 edn., p. 84.

14 *Equality*, p. 50.

15 *Morality, Capitalism and Democracy*, p. 16.

16 *Ibid.*, p. 18.

17 *Ibid.*

18 *Ibid.*, p. 20.

19 *Ibid.*, p. 14.

20 CB, p. 34.

21 *Equality*, p. 228.

22 ESP, p. 22.

23 CB, p. 56.

24 *The Attack and Other Papers*, p. 174.

25 See *A Community of Self Reliance: The New Consensus on Family and Welfare*, a working seminar chaired by Novak, UPA, 1987.

26 *The Economist*, September 8 1990, p. 29ff.

27 *A Community of Self Reliance*, p. 111.

28 See Dobbing, J., (ed.), *Infant Feeding, the Anatomy of a Controversy 1973-1984*, Springer Verlag, 1988, pp. 103-4.

29 *Morality, Capitalism and Democracy*, p. 20.

30 *Ibid*, p. 11.

31 CB, p. 56.

32 Report of the (Sheen) court, No. 8074, Department of Transport, 1987.

33 See Welby, J., *Can Companies Sin?*, Grove Ethical Studies, 1992.

34 See Robinson, S., *Serving Society: The Social Responsibility of Business*, Grove Ethical Studies, 1992.

35 CB, p. 61.

36 See Terrill, R., *R H Tawney and his Times*, Andre Deutsch, 1973, pp. 190-197.

37 *The Acquisitive Society*, Wheatsheaf, 1982 edn., p. 148.

38 A good example of such an analysis is found in Carter, R., 'A Taxonomy of Objectives for Professional Education', *Studies in Higher Education*, 1985, 10(2), pp. 135-149.

The Spirit of Democratic Capitalism: A Critique of Michael Novak

Richard H. Roberts

Introduction

Second only, perhaps, to Pope John-Paul II, Professor Michael Novak is the most influential contemporary Roman Catholic apologist for 'democratic capitalism'. Acting out of character with many of his own generation of theologians and ethicists, Novak has advanced a trenchant defence of the capitalist system in which he contends that whilst this system is not ideal, it is manifestly better than all known alternatives. Moreover, democratic capitalism has an intrinsic and mutually enabling relationship with Christianity and Judaism. Capitalism, however, 'needs a moral theory about itself' and for Novak this theory must also comprise an explicit 'theology of economics', a theology of the capitalist system itself. We designate this conception a 'theology of capitalism' (rather than use Novak's term 'theology of economics') because whilst there are many different forms of economics which could be theologised, *The Spirit of Democratic Capitalism* is explicitly concerned with a specific form of capitalism. In this theology, human beings are understood to experience transcendence in the act of self-creation triggered at the point of encounter with the 'empty shrine' that lies at the heart of the capitalist social order, and they continue their strivings in the 'dark night' of the entrepreneurial soul.

Seen in historical terms, Novak's sympathetic and seductive apology for democratic capitalism, and his associated theology of entrepreneurial strife and striving are necessary correctives to the sustained anti-capitalist polemic of much Christian theology.

Novak's views are therefore most valuable as legitimations of activity in the production and supply side of the economy; but they do not, in this writer's judgement, fully meet the wider (and very complex) demands of a properly contextual theory (and theology) of the economic activity of individuals and communities in the new, post-marxist, globalised and transnational world order. In the following brief exposition and critique of *The Spirit of Democratic Capitalism* we outline and examine some of Novak's claims and then raise a number of fundamental questions that deserve fuller exploration on a scale that cannot be undertaken here.[1]

The Strange Neglect of Capitalism

Michael Novak's intellectual inspiration comes to a marked extent from the French Catholic humanist philosopher Jacques Maritain, who, like Novak, underwent something of a conversion as regards the nature and consequences of capitalism. Maritain conceded in *Integral Humanism*,[2] that his 'proximate ideal' was most closely realised in the American system as he encountered it at first hand in the United States. More comprehensively, Novak maintains that neither Catholic nor Protestant theology has done justice to the 'distinctive theory and practice of the American form of political economy'.[3] Novak relates his own efforts to remedy this democratic deficit to his disenchantment with socialism and his move towards a renewed political realism. In this, he can be regarded as something of a latter-day Catholic Reinhold Niebuhr, who in the course of a lifetime has turned from socialism to a distinctive form of Christian realism. Novak came to understand that he would have to violate the taboo of his generation—and *praise* capitalism. In other words, he converted. He gradually came to the conviction that 'the dream of democratic socialism is inferior to the dream of democratic capitalism'.[4] Having concluded thus, Novak felt impelled to engage in a 'fair examination' of the American system of political economy which is 'perhaps our last, best hope'.[5]

Novak's new realism eschews any ancestral Catholic nostalgia for a lost agrarian and organic pre-industrial age. Thus twentieth century Protestant individualism and Catholic personalism, the

Catholic phenomenologists, even Aquinas and Aristotle, have all, according to Novak, failed to come fully to grips with the 'justice of producing wealth and creating economic development'.[6] In short, Catholic social and economic ethics always focused upon the problem of *distribution* and consistently neglected the sphere of *production*: it is now time for a correction.

To summarise Novak's argument: Christian, and in particular, Catholic thought failed to understand the transformation in the nature and understanding of reality implied by the rise of industrialism. As a consequence of the latter, nature is no longer a static given, but the fecund partner in human productive effort; thus human activity is rightly understood as an immanent creativity that invites comparison with work of the Creator Himself. Productive economic activity takes up its true place as an important analogy with the divine being. Glossing this position, we may say that creation and creativity (with all their *destructive* implications) displace the largely dependent, relational-ethical and passive images and models of much Catholic and post-Enlightenment Protestant theology, and their critiques of, or flights from, capitalism.

In the opening pages of *The Spirit of Democratic Capitalism* Professor Michael Novak points to a pervasive weakness in the history of the Christian Churches' intellectual witness during the last two centuries. Socialism had maintained its spell (as Novak wrote in 1982) *despite* the facts, whereas democratic capitalism has neglected the dimension of vision which is no longer supplied by the moral and cultural leaders of society. Indeed, since the first publication of *The Spirit of Democratic Capitalism* the political collapse of Marxist socialism has followed upon its intellectual and moral decline. The moral and cultural failure to which Novak referred has now in some countries become an abyss analogous in scale and trauma to the crisis in Weimar Germany after the First World War. In broad historical terms, however:

> the churches did not understand the new economics. Officially and through the theologians, they often regarded 'the new spirit of capital-

ism' as materialistic, secular, and dangerous to religion, as in many respects—being in and of the world—it was.[7]

The inability of the church of the time (here Novak would seem to speaking in particular of the Roman Catholic Church, but his comment is more widely applicable) to understand the moral -cultural roots of the new economics was a pivotal failure; but today, insofar as this remains true, such neglect is nothing short of a scandal. Whilst democratic capitalism is to be justified primarily in *practical* terms and not (like socialism) as a *theory*, nevertheless it now desperately needs a moral theory about itself. Capitalism is indispensable, but dangerous; it is essential to human life, yet it threatens the integrity of the cultural foundation upon which it relies. For Novak, religion is integral to this foundation, and it is thus fundamental to his conception of capitalism. Novak's substantial and highly influential book is a bold attempt to correct such systematic neglect and denigration. Many others have sought to explore and clarify the interface between theology and economics; it is, however, Novak's informed and enthusiastic advocacy of capitalism that sets him apart from more cautious thinkers of both this and earlier generations.

'Democratic capitalism': its Definition, Triumph and Travails

By the term 'democratic capitalism' Novak means:

> Three systems in one: a predominantly market economy; a polity respectful of the rights of the individual to life, liberty, and the pursuit of happiness; and a system of cultural institutions moved by ideals of liberty and justice for all.[8]

Novak's presentation is built around the indispensable interconnection of these three 'systems', and it is precisely the problematic relation between these alleged internal necessities and the wide range of contingent and contextual factors that makes both the argument itself and a critical response to it a complex matter. This is not, as Novak frequently points out, solely a theoretical issue but also one of practice. His premise is that:

> In the conventional view, the link between a democratic political system and a market economy is merely a matter of history. My argument is

that the link is stronger: political democracy is compatible in practice only with a market economy. In turn, both systems nourish and are best nourished by a pluralistic liberal culture.[9]

Such a matrix of interconnected factors require for their mutual fulfilment both economic growth and social mobility. Modern capitalism and modern democracy share origins in a common historical epoch and they continue to strengthen each other; their 'logics' are integral, and both also require a 'special moral-cultural base'. Novak's book is ostensibly about the 'life of the spirit which makes democratic capitalism possible'[10] and it is this approach which should alert us. Inspired (not without a touch of irony) by the impulse of Marx's panegyric on the achievements of bourgeois class in the *Communist Manifesto* (1848), Novak presents the reader with an array of facts and figures which illustrate the immense scale and speed of growth at the outset of the industrial era. In this setting, Novak then proposes a threefold approach: first, in Part One, he is to tackle the 'living spirit' of democratic capitalism; in Part Two he examines the countervailing account of what is left of the socialist idea today. In Part Three he outlines in fuller terms the first stirrings of a religious perspective on democratic capitalism. The first part of *The Spirit of Democratic Capitalism* contains an extended examination of the 'underlying moral structures which make the practices of democracy and capitalism work'. According to Novak, there are the following such structures in the ethos of democratic capitalism: 'a special evolution of pluralism; respect for contingency and unintended consequences; a sense of sin; and a new and distinctive conception of community, the individual and the family'.[11] But are these attributes, the reader might ask, a sufficient description of the moral content of capitalism? Furthermore, what are the grounds for accepting Novak's prioritisation of the individual over social structure, in a re-inversion not merely of Marxism in its classic forms, but also of the sociologically-informed practices that manipulate the lives of hundreds of millions of human beings on a daily—and global basis?

Interestingly, Novak's argument is perhaps best understood as *rhetorical* in the classical sense (rather than pragmatic, analytical or theoretical), insofar as he is first concerned to analyse the *ethos* of democratic capitalism in terms of its 'moral structures', or constitutive commonplaces. An apt parallel here might well be the great Adam Smith, whose *Wealth of Nations, Theory of the Moral Sentiments* and posthumously published *Lectures on Rhetoric* were also mutually related aspects of a greater totality.

Ironically, however, since the advent of the 'Thatcher era' in Britain (1979), the rhetoric of naked facticity, repeatedly expressed in the catch-all phrase 'The plain fact of the matter is...' has systematically blocked from the outset the kind of reflective consideration here developed by Novak.[12] The near extinction of an adequate and effective political culture in Britain in the course of the last decade and a half has impeded this mode of enquiry, which at its best is an investigation into the qualities and attributes of the political and social culture of capitalism as it is actually lived on a daily basis.

On the one hand, Professor Novak may also be said to have taken over and inverted the praxis of liberation theology. Thus he begins with an description (analysis would be too strong a designation) of a context which is decidedly not British or indeed West European; it remains in certain respects deeply North American. For Novak, in every setting the fundamental problem to be addressed is nonetheless the same: hatred of, and the self-hatred of capitalism:

> Throughout the world, capitalism evokes hatred. The word is associated with selfishness, exploitation, inequality, imperialism, war.... Democratic capitalism seems to have lost its spirit. To invoke loyalty to it because it brings prosperity seems to some merely materialistic. The Achilles heel of democratic capitalism is that for two centuries now it has appealed so little to the human spirit.[13]

Novak elaborates his overall standpoint which has been much influenced by Daniel Bell and Joseph Schumpeter.[14] Here he shares common concerns with other commentators, not least those of the English Anglican theologian and ethicist V.A. Demant[15] with the corrosive character of capitalism: 'The ironic flaw which such writers discern in democratic capitalism is this: that its successes in the political order and in the economic order undermine it in the cultural order'.[16]

Novak then reviews some of the most common charges made against capitalism: the corruptions of affluence; the exploitation of moral weakness by advertising, structural irresponsibility in political action; the existence of a powerful and adversarial class; the declining status of aristocracy; the role of envy; and 'bourgeois' taste. 'In sum', according to Novak, 'democratic capitalism appears to the orderly eye a morass of cultural contradictions. Not many poets, philosophers, or theologians have smiled kindly upon it. It seethes with adversarial spirit'.[17] So far as Novak is concerned, these problems are part of a price worth paying, for the alternative is a socialistic imposition of a 'better way', an obligatory reimposition of the political and economic realms. Yet, the reader might once more ask, does this somewhat simplistic opposition between accepting either the socio-economic mechanics of capitalism or the imposition of a unified system of cultural values stand up? Does not a humane realism, fully understood, indicate that every situation in which economic forces, social structure, and cultural agency interpenetrate is likely to be far more complex than at first might appear? Is there not, by contrast, an ever-present need for a fully-informed and critical response within each context developed on the basis of the interpenetration of knowledge and power?

Weber and the Deficiencies of Tradition

In answer, as it were, to the demand for more and better theory, Novak reviews ground familiar to those with some knowledge of the history of capitalism. In particular, he invokes Weber's preliminary definition of capitalism in the *Protestant Ethic*:

> Capitalism is identical with the pursuit of profit, and forever renewed profit, by means of continuous, rational, capitalistic enterprise.... A Capitalist economic action...rests on the expectation of profit by the

utilization of opportunities for exchange, that is on (formally) peaceful chances of profit.[18]

The 'chances of profit' issue is vital: without hope of profit there is no likelihood of risk-taking and the commitment of individuals and their resources. As Novak recalls, Weber reviewed six elements in his widened definition of capitalism: free labour; reason; continuous enterprise; separation of home and workplace; stable networks of law; and the primacy of the urban environment. Acknowledging a number of flaws in Weber's account, Novak proposes two corrections and a move beyond the *Protestant Ethic*. In the first instance, Weber failed to analyze the necessary connection between economic liberty and political liberty, a necessity not of logic but of fact. Weber perceived the importance of the link between the *moral* and the *economic*, but he neglected the *political* dimension. The reversion of capitalism to state control in fascism and in collectivist socialism produces a system which is no longer capitalism but the patrimonial state. In the second instance, Novak maintains that Weber misconstrued the practical intelligence in capitalism as 'rational-legal' and thus mechanical, rather than inventive, intuitive and dynamic. Consequently, Weber also misunderstood the insight and practical wisdom required by the entrepreneur and the manager.

In his criticism of Weber, Novak draws upon J.S. Schumpeter whose careful analysis of the role of the entrepreneur[19] occupies a paradigmatic status in post-war discussion. Yet the reader would do well to recall that Schumpeter argued for the increasing obsolescence of the 'entrepreneur' in developed, bureaucratic capitalism. Unlike the 'iron cage' unforgettably depicted in the closing paragraphs of the *Protestant Ethic*, democratic capitalism is inhabited by a multiplicity of styles of rationality. This is, perhaps, a discreet reference on Novak's part to questions raised in recent discussion of the modernity/postmodernity problematic. In other words (but Novak does not use this terminology), advanced capitalism is likely to be 'postmodern' in its appropriation of styles and identities and its valorisation of differentiated rationalities (and irrationalities!) and its correlative repudiation of a 'mechanical' notion of reason and rationality.

Novak resolves the argument on a level of great generality, thereby avoiding the theoretical questions arising in the modern/postmodern debate. Weber's failure also lay in his inability to discern the necessity of cultural pluralism to democratic capitalism: 'a pluralistic spirit decisively distinguishes democratic capitalism from either traditionalist or socialist societies'.[20] Whereas traditional societies and, somewhat ironically, Marxist socialist societies embody a unitary order of moral values, democratic capitalism does not so prescribe its own inner moral essence, except insofar as it makes a principle out of denying the existence or desirability of such a single, unitary essence. Thus an anti-communist cultural conservative like Aleksandr Solhenitsyn can speak of the 'moral poverty' of democratic capitalism, a system which is according to Novak, a 'new order of the world' that does 'not make spiritual purposes central to its inner order'.[21] But these oppositions represent an oversimplified view of the matter: pre-modernity, modernity and post-modernity may co-exist within one country and thus result in dramatically different socio-cultural and 'polity' dynamics within a single overall frame of reference. Simplistic polarities are always liable to be implicit in campaigns of misrepresentation.

Nihilism and the Spirituality of the 'Empty Shrine'

It is at this juncture that Novak's theology of democratic capitalism begins to emerge. The emptiness at the heart of capitalism is not a flaw (as it would seem to be seen from the standpoints of both traditional and socialist conceptions of moral order) but deliberate. Anomie, alienation, loneliness, despair, loss of meaning and so on are 'the necessary other side to any genuine experience of liberty'.[22] This experience is intrinsic to the freedom to conceive culture as *other*: it is a sign of the human capacity for transcendence. In Augustine's words, cited by Novak from the *Confessions*, 'Our hearts are restless, Lord, until they find their rest in Thee'. Likewise, St John of the Cross himself teaches us that the freedom to learn involves a painful process of detachment. Thus whilst

Novak appeals to Peter Berger's idea of the 'sacred canopy', this is too positive and too unified a metaphor to represent what is taking place. Berger's other, more hesitant expression, 'signs of transcendence' might better encapsulate Novak's conception of religious experience in a pluralist culture and society:

> In a genuinely pluralist society, there is no one sacred canopy. By intention there is not. At its spiritual core, there is an empty shrine. that shrine is left empty in the knowledge that no one word, image, or symbol is worthy of what all seek there. Its emptiness, therefore, represents the transcendence which is appropriated by free consciences from a virtually infinite number of directions.... Believer and unbeliever, selfless and selfish, frightened and bold, naive and jaded, all participate in an order whose center is not imposed.[23]

In a distinctive sense 'transcendence' is entrenched in the Declaration of Independence and the Constitution of the United States. Such phrases as 'in God we trust' and the notion of inalienable rights endowed by the Creator imply the legal and the societal embodiment and enactment, but not the definition, of 'God'. Indeed, Novak argues, 'These words are like pointers, which each person must define for himself' and 'their function is to protect the liberty of conscience of all, by using a symbol which transcends the power of the state and any other earthly power'.[24] There is thus an inescapable role for transcendence at the heart of democratic capitalism, an open emptiness that invites—even compels—constant re-definition. Theology is *not* marginal but central (despite secularisation) to Novak's conception of the capitalist process. This emptiness impels progress and deflates utopian dreams; but the possibility, indeed the necessity of constant improvement (and progress) is entrenched:

> The moral progress to which democratic capitalism calls is not utopian; but it is never at an end in history. The fact that the centre is kept empty does not mean that it lacks vitality, but rather that its vitality exceeds the limits of any one instrument by which its nature might be adequately defined'.[25]

Here is a challenging conception which invites depiction in terms of what Ernst Bloch would have called 'forward-dawning consciousness'. How well equipped are religions (especially traditional and 'established') to meet such requirements? It is interesting to note the ambiguities in the Jewish Marxist Ernst Bloch's treatment of the 'American Dream' which is embedded in a formal a-theology as pervasive as Novak's own theology.[26] As regards the United States, the practical, rather than a credal 'sacred canopy' allows for 'unity in practice, diversity in belief'. So Novak argues that both traditional and socialist societies offer, in fact impose, unitary visions, and thereby seek to suffuse every social activity with symbolic solidarity in answer to the needs of a primal form of human hunger. In democratic capitalism:

> Atavistic needs haunt each free person. The 'wasteland' at the heart of democratic capitalism is like a field of battle, on which individuals wander alone, in some confusion, amid many casualties. Nonetheless, like the dark night of the soul in the inner journey of the mystics, this desert has an indispensable purpose. It is maintained out of respect for the diversity of human consciences, perceptions, and intentions. It is swept clean out of reverence for the sphere of the transcendent, to which the individual has access through the self, beyond the mediations of social institutions. The domain of the transcendent, of course, is mediated by literature, religion, family, and fellows. But it is finally centered in the silence in each person.[27]

This is the ambiguous nub of Novak's argument where the demand for self-transcendence implicit in capitalism encounters the historically and culturally mediated forms of transcendence in a plural, even multi-cultural society. Here liberty is contextualised and entrenched in a conception of pluralist order which by design violates the unitary orders (and anti-individualism) of traditional and socialist societies:

> Democratic capitalism not only permits individuals to experience alienation, anomie, loneliness, and nothingness. Democratic capitalism is also constantly renewed by such radical experiences of human liberty...humans are not, in the end, fully plumbed by the institutions in which they dwell. Each experiences a solitariness and personal responsi-

bility which renders him (or her) oddly alone in the midst of solidarity. Conscience is the taproot of democratic capitalism. It is so because individuals are capable of the experience of nothingness—that is, able to raise questions about all schemes of community, order, purpose, and meaning, and able to choose in darkness—that individuals have inalienable rights. Democratic capitalism respects this transcendence by limiting its own reach.[28]

Such a characterisation of capitalism could appear at first glance to confirm the impression that objective nihilism might in fact underlie all human experience in capitalist society. Novak attempts to counter this general impression by drawing attention to the indispensability of the 'moral culture' that must service the needs of capitalism. Democratic capitalism is not 'a free enterprise system alone' for 'it cannot thrive apart from the moral culture that nourishes the virtues and values on which its existence depends'.[29] The situation is, of course, more complex than this statement might suggest; but in the final analysis the choice (according to Novak) might well have to be between either allowing the capitalist impulse off its leash—and then striving to re-capture it, or constraining it *ab initio* at the cost of poverty and paralysis. We may regard the societal experiment of the Thatcher era in Britain as an important example of such an unleashing. But in Britain there remains an unresolved tension between a fragile (now largely extinct) entrepreneurial (innovative) conception of capitalism as 'enterprise culture' and the practice of an invasive, centralised bureaucratic hegemony, extended, in the guise of 'privatisation', over all sectors of society.

Novak's account comes perilously close to lending substance to the views of those who regard the social and moral order of capitalism as irretrievably nihilistic, a view now criticised (and sometimes caricatured) by feminist theoreticians. The elaboration of a 'theology of economics' later in *The Spirit of Democratic Capitalism* is decorative in comparison with the author's initial and unflinching recognition of a vital nihilism at the core of capitalism and the consequent overwhelming need for the constant re-creation of human identity and legitimation.

It is here that the contextual character of Novak's argument is once more apparent. Manifestly capitalist 'free enterprise' countries like Brazil have to be disallowed. Rather like socialist disputes about 'real socialism', so Novak is obliged to engage in a selectivity exercise in order to restrict his argument to examples of proper or real forms of democratic capitalism. It is at this juncture that the 'moral culture' finds itself under acute strain, once ethical expectations are contrasted with what actually happens in capitalist countries (even 'democratic' ones):

> Democratic capitalism is not a free enterprise system merely. Its political system has many legitimate roles to play in economic life, from protecting the soundness of the currency to regulating international trade and internal competition. Its moral-cultural system also has many legitimate and indispensable roles to play in economic life, from encouraging self-restraint, hard work, discipline, and sacrifice for the future to insisting upon generosity, compassion, integrity, and concern for the common good. The economic activist is simultaneously a citizen of the polity and a seeker after truth, beauty, virtue, and meaning'.[30]

The latter statement might well now occasion some scepticism on the part of those who have escaped the immediate consequences of the activities of Ivan Bowsky, the directors of BCCI, the late Robert Maxwell and the present British Chancellor of the Exchequer, to name but a few. Who could endorse the foregoing paragraph without severe, even crippling doubts about the 'realism' of Novak's conception of 'sin'? Novak strains credulity in the face of social facts. The 'sin' that he regards as central to the self-understanding of democratic capitalism is far more pervasive and deep-rooted than he allows. A more sensitive and nuanced sociology and anthropology of contextual factors is required. An effective contextual theology of capitalism would not merely rehabilitate something of the order of Niebuhr's 'Christian realism' alone, but also recognise in fuller theoretical terms that the basis of 'sin' is both individual and structural.

The Spirit of Democratic Capitalism continues with an extended review of some basic features of democratic capitalism, and this is followed by a critique of liberation theology. Novak concludes with a 'Theology of Economics' in which he recasts in a preliminary way the doctrines of the Trinity and the Incarnation. These considerations are rounded off with rehabilitations of the ideas of competition, original sin, the separation of realms, and *caritas* (the word 'love' having been abused beyond linguistic redemption). Near the end of *The Spirit of Democratic Capitalism* Novak states what he considers to be the most profound and intractable problem affecting the evaluation of capitalism:

> The problem for a system of economy is how to unleash human creativity and productivity whilst coping realistically with human sinfulness. To love humans as they are is to accept them in their sinfulness, while seeking a way to transform such sinfulness into creative action for the commonweal. Some argue that the best way to do this is to appeal to social solidarity and high moral ideals. They erect economic systems accordingly. Others hold that the common good is better served through allowing each individual to work as each judges best and to keep the rewards of their labor. For them, the profit motive is designed to inspire a higher level of common benefit by respecting the individual judgment of economic agents. the more the latter risk and invest, the greater return they will gather in. Most will not be selfish with this return; most will share it liberally.[31]

Would that the latter sentiments might be true—but for the most part they are not justified by the evidence. This is optimism which few (other than those in whose interests it was to concur) would endorse. Novak here provides us with what amounts to a quasi-soteriology grounded in the capitalist delivery of humankind from mere subsistence into creativity and the abundant productivity, that issues, so we are encouraged to believe, in universal benefit. All of this is based upon premises that do not fully enough recognise the conditions of human emergence in the sphere of economic activity. We have to ask if Professor Novak is in fact truly an inhabitant of the real worlds we inhabit, and whether, furthermore, he is still prepared to pay the price necessary for the maintenance of the system of democratic capitalism, which now since 1989-90 in effect rules the world (albeit imperfectly).

Conclusion

Novak concludes his treatise, as ever, upon an optimistic and explicitly theological note:

> Almighty God did not make creation coercive, but designed it as an arena of liberty. Within that arena, God has called for individuals and peoples to live according to His law and inspiration. Democratic capitalism has been designed to permit them, sinners all, to follow this free pattern. It creates a noncoercive society as an arena of liberty, within which individuals and peoples are called to realize, through democratic methods, the vocations to which they believe they are called.[32]

Novak confronts us with an uncompromising and neo-romantic revitalisation of the 'protestant ethic' in the distinctively North American form of a theology of capitalism. Novak's presentation attempts morally to endorse an economic system that has 'triumphed', certainly for the moment, over socialism; yet his apologia does not escape the possibility of damaging criticism. We conclude our consideration of *The Spirit of Democratic Capitalism* with some observations, both critical and positive.

Novak's argument draws for its apparent universalisability upon contextual factors that are in fact relative. There are a number of aspects of this relativism, but some of the most obvious concern the role of labour and markets under conditions that are not 'natural' except in primitive and ideal conditions. Markets are usually struggles between unequal participants (i.e. in national, ethnic, gender, hereditary, or 'capital' terms) that take place in diverse contexts. Whilst these disparities are global, they also increasingly occur in parts of highly-developed societies like the United States and Britain. At the heart of this problem lies the emergence of large, socially and economically redundant sectors of societies, designated as an 'underclass' whose representatives do not function as effective (i.e. culturally 'empowered') participants in the market.

This deculturated sector of society is now becoming significantly disfunctional and absorbed, to an extent as yet undetermined, into a culture of arbitrary violence. Ironically, an underclass group exhibits all too clearly the anomie and alienation that Novak sees as intrinsic to capitalism. But an underclass, facing the apparent prospect of its social redundancy in the likely future labour markets of advanced industrial society, does not (indeed cannot) necessarily appropriate to itself that economically-beneficial striving towards transcendence central to Novak's conception of democratic capital- ism. In such a setting, religious hope *may* operate as absolute resistance to absolute despair; but hope as reasonable expectation based on the discernment and appropriation of life-chances is something other than the former. Below a certain level of participation the effort/outcomes equation is such as to defeat hope. For the first time in British industrial history an indigenous religious hope inherited through Christian tradition (above all in the form of Methodism) has disappeared from the horizon of a significant, indeed a dominant proportion of the population. As hopelessness and low esteem gain a grip, so resignation may no longer appease anger, and a conversion to evil may come about. There is such a thing as a no-start situation. Resistance to despair and the transformation of hope into planning require the systematic investment of human resources and of all forms of 'capital'. Incitement to enter unaided the free market is not enough.

What might then be involved in the creation/re-creation of labour forces capable of competing in the European/world labour market? What are the rights of those in a consumerist culture who are drawn into a militant subculture that subsists largely outside the sphere of legitimate economic activity and socialisation of civil society? Such questions can only be answered satisfactorily, if at all, through very careful scrutiny of what the French sociologist Pierre Bourdieu has apostrophised as the distribution of 'cultural' or 'intellectual capital'. Entry to known and likely future labour markets will depend directly upon the possession of relevant forms of such capital. A theology of capitalism which fails to absorb such arguments will remain external to the reality of those ensnared in underclass status, the new tribalism of a homegrown, indigenous

'Ik'; a reality which we refuse to acknowledge and articulate in its full horror at the cost of gross injustice—and our own peril.

Michael Novak has challenged the Christian Churches to pay serious attention to the reality and legitimacy of economic activity. In response however, we must go further and deeper than he does if we are both to radicalize and Christianise critical engagement with the fundamental human right to engage in economic creativity. Novak has pointed the way towards a renewal of such exploration. At the level of theological reflection an adequate 'theology' of capitalism would require a 'thick', as opposed to a 'thin' representation of human life as it exists under contemporary capitalism. The essential respect for persons fundamental to a Christian view of life will therefore have to be functionalised in the creation of a social and cultural vision of the human condition grounded in research rather than fantasy. On this bedrock of recognition of actual state of the 'other' (and of our mutual obligations as citizens) the call to create wealth would not mock and enrage poverty and incapacity. It would, on the contrary, serve to provoke and promote responsible economic participation within an informed understanding of ecological outcomes—but that is another story.

Notes

1   Roberts, Richard, H., *Religion and the Resurgence of Capitalism*, forthcoming December 1993, London: Routledge.

2   Maritain, Jacques, Evans, Joseph, W., trans., *Integral Humanism*, New York: 1978.

3   Novak, Michael, *The Spirit of Democratic Capitalism*, London: Institute of Economic Affairs Health and Welfare Unit, 2nd Edition, 1991, p. 21.

4   Novak, *op. cit.*, p. 26.

5   Novak, *op. cit.*, p. 28.

6   Novak, *op. cit.*, pp. 24-5.

7   Novak, *op. cit.*, p. 17.

8   Novak, *op. cit.*, p. 14.

9 Novak, *op. cit.*, p. 14.

10 Novak, *op. cit.*, p. 16.

11 Novak, *op. cit.*, p. 29.

12 Roberts, Richard, H., 'Religion and the "Enterprise Culture": The British Experience in the Thatcher Era 1979-1990', *Social Compass*, 39 (1), 1992, pp. 15-33.

13 Novak, *op. cit.*, p. 31.

14 Bell, D., *The Cultural Contradictions of Capitalism*, New York: 1978; Schumpeter, J.A., *Capitalism, Socialism and Democracy*, 1943, pp. 142ff.

15 Demant, V.A., *Religion and the Decline of Capitalism*, Oxford: 1949.

16 Novak, *op. cit.*, p. 31.

17 Novak, *op. cit.*, p. 35.

18 Weber, Max, Giddens, Anthony, (ed), *The Protestant Ethic and the Spirit of Capitalism*, New York: 1978, p. 91.

19 Schumpeter, J.A. *Capitalism, Socialism and Democracy*, 1943, pp. 130ff.

20 Novak, *op. cit.*, p.49.

21 Novak, *op. cit.*, p. 51.

22 Novak, *op. cit.*, p. 52.

23 Novak, *op. cit.*, p. 53.

24 Novak, *op. cit.*, p. 54.

25 Novak, *op. cit.*, p. 54.

26 Roberts, Richard, H., *Hope and Its Hieroglyph: A Critical Decipherment of Ernst Bloch's 'Principle of Hope'*, Atlanta: Scholars Press, 1989.

27 Novak, *op. cit.*, p. 55.

28 Novak, *op. cit.*, p. 55.

29 Novak, *op. cit.*, p. 56.

30 Novak, *op. cit.*, pp. 57-58.

31 Novak, *op. cit.*, p. 356.

32 Novak, *op. cit.*, pp. 359-60.

Section Two:
Capitalism With A Theology?

The Wolf, the Goat and the Lettuce
The Church and the European Model of Political Economy

John Kennedy

Nobility tempers sovereignty, and draws the eyes of the people somewhat aside from the line royal. But for democracies, they need it not, and they are commonly quieter and less subject to sedition than where there are families of nobles. For men's eyes are on the business, and not upon the persons; or if upon the persons, it is for the business' sake, as for the fittest, and not for flags and pedigree. We see the Switzers last well, not withstanding their diversity of religion and of cantons; for utility is their bond, not respects. The United Provinces of the Low Countries in their government excel; for where there is an equality, the consultations are more impartial, and the payment and tributes more cheerful.[1]

Francis Bacon: on nobility

Prosperity is the blessing of the Old Testament, adversity is the blessing of the New.[2]

Francis Bacon: on adversity

These are our texts for a modest exposition on 'God and the Marketplace'. We turn to them later. First to set out more directly the problem which they obliquely address.

The market is enormously important in the fulfilment of human needs and purposes. It has also suffered persistent criticism from the Church through the ages. This judgement, often justified, continues today. Such judgement is often misplaced, however. Not only that, but the criticisms are launched from the wrong location. In brief, the Church is working with an inadequate model of how society functions. (By 'the Church' is generally meant that area of the churches in which time and thought are devoted to developing material on social issues—a relatively limited fraction of the whole People of God. Other senses will be evident from the context.)

This paper seeks to draw together elements of a model of political economy which might help us be more rigorous, realistic and effective in our political theology. The notions to be laid out are simple and familiar. They describe a contemporary form of European political economy which is not simply capitalist, but a complex of institutions which comprise what is called here *the Human Republic*. These notions have become commonplace in the discussion of the nature of European politics, but they have yet to make a serious imprint on the process of political theology, where much otherwise excellent work seems to be based on an over-simple model of political economy. The difficulty seems essentially one of handling experience in the theological context.

Theology and Experience

The 17th Century Anglican theologian Richard Hooker has given us a useful formula for locating the place of Scripture in theological discourse. Scripture, he said, takes its place alongside the Christian tradition and the capacity to reason. The Methodists at some later stage added the matter of religious experience; at some point this addition has been modified to refer to all the experience of human life. This is not necessarily the best way to do theology, but it does help reveal one of the rather veiled problems in the field, particularly in political theology; that the mass of human experience cannot simply be appended to such a list. Experience overlies the earlier categories, so that the traditional categories themselves are a barely legible palimpsest. The mass of contemporary experience confuses by its mass and change; the meaning of the traditional theological material which it now obscures is difficult to recover.

The temptation is to reduce experience to something that more easily accords with the conventional theological categories, rather than giving full weight to the inconvenient material of real life. Such a temptation lies clearly across the subject at issue here, 'God and the Marketplace'. It is, for instance, convenient to accept the implication that the market might be regarded as some kind of free-standing entity. There is, of course, no such thing as a free market, and it is mistaken to imagine that when we are talking about economics we are addressing the real issues of political economy. Markets always stand in some political context, never more so than in our current European setting.

The recent Anglo-American obsession with the virtues of unfettered capitalism threatens to draw the Church into an unreal debate, but one which conveniently reduces the complexity of the material of human experience. Examples multiply almost daily. Pope John Paul's remarkable *Centesimus Annus*[3] has been so drawn. It reminds us eloquently that while labour is a commodity, people are not things. Yet capitalism is given an ontological status that it just doesn't have. Richard Harries, Bishop of Oxford, has served us well with his reinterpretation of Richard Niebuhr; yet he too in a recent work[4] has tackled the merits and faults of a free-standing capitalism that just do not exist. Even Ronald Preston has been drawn into calling his recent excellent book *Religion and the Ambiguities of Capitalism*[5], though the content addresses the issues with great wisdom. Donald Hay's splendid *Economics Today*[6] gives a clear and succinct description of the weaknesses of capitalist and socialist models of political economy, but does not move on to an account of the model upon which our own polity is based. It would be impertinent to suggest great failings in these works, but there is a tendency to isolate the market from the totality of political economy. The work considered as a whole does rather suggest a conversation that is not quite starting.

There is, however, at least one simple, readable demolition of the notion of the market as a free-standing entity, and which describes a more true to life model—John Gray's *The Moral Foundations of Market Institutions*.[7] Gray gives a subtle account of a model of political economy that takes note of the whole experience of a contemporary European polity, essentially similar to what follows.

The Human Republic

We take our starting point somewhat more remotely than Gray does, in order to set the market not only in political but in historical context. We start with Francis Bacon's no doubt distorted perceptions of the Swiss and Dutch polities.

In this extraordinary paragraph, Bacon lays out the elements of a model of political economy. Where the people are governed by consent, and prosper through business, peace reigns. Not least important to a former Lord Chancellor, equality makes political debate easier, taxes are yielded cheerfully, and public purposes are therefore easier of achievement. This passage is important not only because it can be forced into a particular framework; there is a crucially important aspect of sensibility here. Bacon sees the behaviour of these foreigners at a distance, morally as well as physically. The hierarchical political system, on whose precarious peak he once perched, is totally different. It requires for him a certain degree of imagination to step into a quite other world, no matter how briefly. (Certainly the concept of the cheerful taxpayer is richly imaginative.) It will be suggested below that a somewhat similar sensibility tends to compromise the Church in its attempt to understand the market and its context.

Bacon is right to spot the Dutch as of special significance. Fernand Braudel[8] recounts endlessly for us the doings of the earlier traders of Europe and the world, but 17th Century Holland is the first self-conscious trading nation—the first human republic in the terms that we will discuss below.

In its term of three generations, it never quite managed to be the Republic of God, however. It is not that trade failed to be more or less moral; it was that it could never be appropriately ordered to correspond to any ecclesial vision of a divine order. Or rather, which is not the same, its disorders were too evident and revealed; teeming, rumbustious, undirected by any serious principle, no matter how serious and principled its participants, too open to an undefined future. Simon Schama lays all this out in great style, and offers us a crucial insight into the nature of the citizen of this republic:

> At the centre of the Dutch world was a burgher, not a bourgeois. There is a difference, and it is more than a nuance of translation. For the

burgher was a citizen first and homo oeconomicus second. So that if any one obsession linked together their several concerns with family, the fortunes of state, the power of their empire, and the condition of their poor, their standing in history and the uncertainties of geography; it was the moral ambiguity of good fortune.[9]

This is just, of course, what Bacon imagined; it is in that civic sense that the term 'bourgeois' is sparingly used below. So we seek to explicate what is implied in Bacon and illustrated in the Holland of his time—the notion of the bourgeois state, the Human Republic.

It may be claimed that there has been established in Europe a modest fulfilment of the early Dutch promise; an institutional ensemble which sustains an innovative market, free politics and an expensive, tax-funded system of social development. The earnest North European nature of this claim needs to be tested throughout against a typically sceptical Italian proverb, directed at anyone who urges any imaginative scheme for the improvement of humanity; 'He says he'll save the wolf, the goat and the lettuce.' We consider the elements of this ensemble in turn.

The Market

It is easy to reify the market; for it to be seen as a cluster of stalls in a town square, or as a group of fat men in top hats watering down the workers' beer. But the market is a process, not a thing. It is the process of finding out how things are best done. It makes the successful wealthy, and provides the customers of the success-ful with at least modest prosperity. The market operates through a myriad of more or less shrewd guesses about what works. Those who guess right get rich; those who guess wrong go broke. The market is the plan that works, through the vast complex of competitive estimates as to what the market will bear, today and tomorrow.

We are in danger here of straying into the area of romance, of conjuring up a figure of fantasy—the clear-eyed, square-jawed, fearless, ruthless, all-seeing entrepreneur. It may be more useful to think of most entrepreneurs as short, fat, bald and scared—less Gordon Gecko, more Mr Magoo. As the old saying goes: 'What most businessmen want most is to be second.' So the market nudges fearfully in the direction of what seems to work, and the whole mass of players get it more or less right. Away from the mass are some more interesting people, but they mainly go broke very quickly, so are seldom heard of. A very few in these high-risk areas make it work, and then the whole mass moves their way. But even in these days of huge concentrations of research, we don't know what these folk are up to, and nor do they most of the time.

This is a homespun way of talking about an important feature of Gray's work—his use of Michael Polanyi's notion of *tacit knowledge*. This is the kind of knowledge which an English merchant banker has of Mozambique and Czechoslovakia, though it is impossible to draw him or her into a conversation about political economy. This is what a Malayalee trader knows about how things work in Madras. Such knowledge is not readily susceptible to intellectual discourse, but it makes the business world go round. This is not to deny that business is immensely technical, organised, forward planning, demanding. It is just that the kind of knowledge which makes it work is odd.

So—it is the teeming mass of the market, the haphazard nature of innovation, and the peculiar form of tacit knowledge, that characterise the market. It is impossible, in principle, to know in advance what will succeed in the marketplace, because it is impossible to know in advance what will constitute success. It is this openness to the future that is one of the market's most distinctive and morally disturbing features. Some of the more commonplace demons of the marketplace might be usefully exorcised at this point.

The market is not essentially exploitative. A growing market economy needs customers, and has no vested interest in their poverty. Quite the reverse—the butcher and the baker's interest tends to be served if their customers are prosperous. The market does not eliminate greed, ambition and vanity from the world, but it does compel the greedy and the ambitious to compete openly with others by lawful means.

The market is, of course, essentially competitive. It is competition that constitutes the market's openness to the future. But the market is not to be described as competitive in some sense that excludes co-operation. As the market becomes more sophisticated, so the combinations of skill, capital and imagination become more complex, and enterprise comes to depend on cooperation. Thus, most people who work for a large, industrial concern never get very close to the competitive edge of the business, but the sharpness of that edge will depend very much on the capacity of those employees to work creatively together.

Just in passing, it is not entirely clear why the useful technique of competition has been elevated into a philosophy of competitiveness. Nothing bedevils discussion of the market so much as its domination by the 'Kick Ass' school of business ethics. It seems to be a feature of mature capitalism that employees are cherished as valuable resources, and that today's competitor is likely to be tomorrow's collaborator.

Markets do not specially hurt the poor. Wherever there are poor people, by definition whatever is going on has hurt them. It seems hardly necessary to say this, but so much Christian rhetoric is bound up in the notion that the market is alright for us, but not for them. This noble sentiment just doesn't square with reality. A poor victim of what Michael Novak[10] calls 'premodern wretchedness' would be no richer in 1700 than in 1600, nor expect to be. Nobody has less access to the market in 1992 than he or she did in 1892, unless that access has been politically denied. For instance, families of semi-skilled workers in the London Borough of Tower Hamlets have much greater access to the private goods supplied by Asda and Tesco than they have to the public goods, like access to employment through education and training, and public housing. That's why they move to Essex if they can, and vote the way they do when they get there.

Further, concern at the contrast between general market-led prosperity and the hardships of the poor must not ignore the historical problem of population and poverty. Between the promise and the execution of Adam Smith's vision falls the shadow of Thomas Malthus. It is true that the first fruit of prosperity is a dramatic drop in the death rates of babies and their mothers; it is also true that the resulting increase in population tends to gobble up the increase in prosperity. The controversial issue of population and poverty in history are vigorously discussed by Braudel,[11] and in Gertrude Himmelfarb's essays on Smith and Malthus.[12]

So—markets select good performers, and give best value to consumers. This is a modest but important achievement. The market has not saved our souls, but it has given us comfort, useful work, health and leisure in measures unimaginable to any other age. It might also claim, to have replaced conflict with competition—and a wide degree of cooperation.

One important feature of this increased prosperity is the manner in which citizens relate to the market less as producers, and more as consumers. One product of the market has been leisure—in large part leisure to consume in the marketplace rather than merely to produce there. The market itself has produced, almost as a minor byproduct, a major cultural artefact to occupy the new leisure area—television. This medium in itself is designed to convey powerful messages about consuming.

A further indirect product of prosperity has been longevity. The fastest-growing area of the market is in the deployment of savings which enable retired producers to maintain a reasonable level of comfort. These savings are the main fuel of the market; they provide one generation of producers with secure retirement and their children with the prospect of work and income. This income is always expected to be greater than that of the previous generation, and these gains are achieved by applying savings to innovation, improvement of productivity and therefore higher capacity to add value. The market has thus allayed the two great fears of millions of people, beside which *timor mortis* is mild indeed; that they will die in poverty, and that their children will be poorer than they. There is a here a kind of consumption-in-depth, which consists of a very widespread acquisition of fairly modest levels of wealth, largely directed towards security in old age. It is therefore misleading to imagine consumption in the marketplace as totally that of environment-destroying junk as advertised on television—except that TV is increasingly taken up with advertising pension plans.

So, the market works better than we tend to give credit for, but it always works in a political context.

The Market in Political Context

In Bacon's time, the political context might be regarded as hostile to a reasonably free operation of the market. This was particularly tragic in Bacon's case; he was perpetually in debt, which could not be relieved by any ignoble means, as for instance writing for the stage. Instead he stole, or was framed for so doing, and was sacked for it. Today he would be a brilliant explainer of absolutely everything on TV. Adam Smith is the classic formulator of what in Bacon is a flashing insight—of a society in which people are largely concerned with business, and not with rank.

It would be a serious mistake to suppose that Smith had no use for the likes of Bacon; he cares little for nobility, but values government. He sees three functions for government; two of them can be taken to stand for the whole libertarian package of political rights. First, there is the duty to protect society from invaders, and second to protect every member of society from criminals. One at least quasi-criminal activity which the state must protect the public against is the avoidance of competition. The key to the market as a public good is competition, but only an entrepreneur of saintly obedience to his calling would go out looking for it; as Smith says, the entrepreneur is a natural conspirator against competition. This has always been the great weakness of the neat market theory: that the virtue of the market rests on its inhabitants doing the one thing they absolutely abhor. The moral foundation of the market is therefore inevitably a strong state. It is this corollary that buries forever the idea of a virtuous 'free' market.

Smith's third function of government is described famously thus:

The duty of erecting and maintaining certain public works and public institutions, which it can never be for the interest of any individual or small number of individuals to erect and maintain, because the profit could never repay the expense to any individual or so small a number of individuals, though it may frequently do more than repay it to a great society'.[13]

Even worse, Smith insists that capitalism oppresses the workers; the industrial division of labour so dulls the worker that,

...he becomes as stupid and ignorant as it is possible for a human creature to become... But in every improved and civilised society this is the state into which the labouring poor, that is, the great body of the people, must necessarily fall, unless government take some pains to prevent it.[14]

It is not entirely perverse to present Smith as an imaginer of the modern corporate state; but he is so only because he is a citizen of the Republic of the Enlightenment, not altogether alien from the Roman republic imagined by Gibbon as the origin of serious concern about the public thing. So let us now talk about the state's role as a serious partner to the market.

The Enabling State

Smith leaves room for the Government to do lots of things and to pay for them. Indeed, Western European countries have converged remarkably on an extraordinary expansion of public expenditure; this ranged from an extreme low of 38 per cent of GNP in Britain in 1990 to 57 per cent in Sweden, with an average of around 46 per cent. (It is of great interest to note that these two countries have since been forced closer to that mean. It is also important to observe that public expenditure figures for the United States and Japan are lower than Britain's; with disastrous consequences, it could be argued, for the first.)

This expenditure pays for education, health care, housing, training, research and development, retirement pensions and minimum living standards for the poorest. So there seems to be a consensus that *the market is inadequate to meet almost half our needs.*

It is clear that such vast expenditure is not concerned merely with the needs of the poor, though much of it is; it sustains every aspect of society, including the ability to perform well in the market. We have here not simply systems of *social welfare*, but systems of *social investment*.

Obviously considerable power is exercised by the institutions that operate these systems. It is naive to think of them as being merely subservient to the popular will as expressed through political institutions; it is therefore useful to think of the enabling state as an institutional ensemble at least as autonomous and complex as the market.

In accepting the role of the enabling state, however, it is necessary to remember how badly the state tends to do things; the likelihood of any single body hitting on the best way to do something, and keeping on getting it right, is remote. Best, then, that the state look around for whoever is doing things best, and pays them to do it. Best too that authority to do the looking is devolved to as local a level as possible, where the taxes to pay for the services are actually collected.

But this barely functional view of the enabling role of the state will not quite do. Smith's nightmare of the dully mechanical mechanic requires that we think of the State as a possible actor in an important field—that of lively and enlivening *belonging*. Our autonomy in the market place is dulled and diminished if the buildings surrounding it are shabby and the public space cramped and ugly. Gray talks of:

> Those inherently public goods that are associated with a public culture in which autonomous individuals have a rich array of options and amenities to chose from..Autonomy is not worth much if it is exercised in a Hobbesian state of nature.[15]

Gray is thinking somewhat wishfully in wanting all this to be got rather cheaply, however—for something under 30 per cent of GNP. The fault seems to lie in his notion of an enabling *welfare* state; this term carries the implication that welfare is the fundamental category of state intervention, whereas that enabling function which actually engages in *social investment* obviates some of the need for welfare. For instance, British proportions of state expenditure were significantly lower than Germany's for some years, but now approach German levels. It could be argued that we are now burdened with public expenditure levels arising from a previous refusal to engage in social investment. It follows that the enabling state probably cannot be got cheaper than around 40 per cent of GNP. Much less and we perpetrate the sham predicted in the Italian proverb: what we have is a wolf, impersonating a goat not eating a lettuce.

Hanging Together

Now we have a basic model of political economy, involving the market, democratic politics and the enabling state. It is important to note how these institutions work together. Social investment helps us to get into a fast-changing labour market and to stay healthy there. The revenues generated by the market sustain social investment. Democratic institutions police free markets, and set acceptable levels of taxation which ensure that the enabling state is maintained. And it must be clearly noted that in this model, market success is as dependent on the enabling state as any other sector of society.

What we have here is a basic model for a republic. Nobody is absolutely in charge, because each institution has a certain autonomy, arising from the general judgement as to who does what best. And quite emphatically, the government does not sit atop the dungheap. There is a public logic that dictates how institutions interact, which it is the function of Government to articulate, but not dictate.

This is the basic ensemble that invites our criticism and engagement. There is, indeed, plenty to criticise, and the brickbats need to be handed out even-handedly. The arrangements can work badly. The operators of the free market may dominate the political institutions, and inhibit the necessary levels of social investment. The enabling state may encroach upon the market, destroy its disciplines in the name of social justice, and wind up an inflationary spiral through index-linked salaries and pensions. The political institutions may close down the market in political ideas by sustaining unrepresentative, secretive and unchecked government.

Indeed, this is the grim view of British society adopted particularly by Europhile British Social Democrats. David Marquand is the most persistently articulate of these. Marquand suggests a model of political economy somewhat like that of the above, speaking of the enabling state as the 'developmental state'.[16] He sketches well the general pattern of British national politics, in which the electorate have till recently been offered the choice between one party that hates business and another party which hates taxes —when the trick, of course, is to get the two to work together.

Marquand develops now-familiar themes with some persuasive power. He describes a society locked in the commercial and political attitudes of a 19th century seaborne empire, which was failing even in its own time. He is especially hard on the British parliamentary tradition, and its imposition on society of a political culture which assumes that:

> Democratic politics revolve round a competitive struggle for the peoples' vote...and that the victors in that struggle are entitled to make what use they wish of the power placed in their hands'.[17]

The European model of political economy is useful in exposing a further significant failing in social relations. We have seen that the notion of the enabling state has superseded that of the welfare state. But it can be argued that this change has operated against the interests of those whom the Welfare State existed to benefit—the poor. The great areas of service provision funded by the enabling state are those of education and health care. It is widely agreed that our education system enables the majority of young people to begin on a life-long career of full-time employment. But it is also clear that this is no longer true for up to a third of our young people. The reasons for this are complex; they involve a tradition of cheerful antipathy to education among those who formerly expected a rough and ready but reasonably secure lifetime in unskilled employment. Those days have gone, but attitudes and educational practices have not yet changed. Yet the parents have paid for a system of education that has not greatly benefited their children.

Similarly in health; the Black Report[18] and *Faith in the City*[19] pointed up the disparities in health and effective health care as between the poor and the normally prosperous. It is clear that not only are health care resources unfairly directed; the health needs of the poor have much more to do with expenditures on housing and availability of employment. Since 1980, investment in social housing has dropped dramatically and unemployment has risen to previously unthinkable and apparently permanent levels.

Somewhat differently there arises the issue of benefits and tax relief. There is a perfectly good logic behind the desire to target the poorest with resources, and even for ignoring the low take-up rate for such benefits on the principle of 'caveat receptor'—it's up to the potential recipient to actualise receipt. But this is hard to square with the open ended subsidy of tax relief enjoyed by the prosperous. The issue can be explored at length in Goodin and Le Grand[20] or as briefly summarised in George.[21] The otherwise judicious Gray has a purple passage on this theme:

> With the exception of a few of its programmes, the British welfare state is a middle class racket without ethical justification or standing, and which (because of its vast transaction costs and wastefulness) does not in the end even benefit the middle classes.[22]

The point is this. It has been suggested above that the poor may not be penalised in the marketplace. What is at issue here is the gross inequality in the enabling state's distribution of resources. This is so thoroughly the case that for a large minority of the population, it is better described as the 'disabling state'—they pays their money and don't get their choice. The model of political economy described here invites us to criticise the public policy elements of this failure, and to examine the dynamics within the enabling state itself which lead to these outcomes.

At this point, the uneasy feeling arises that this exposition may be counterproductive. To see the British situation in the framework of this model is to experience a kind of terror that it's all too awful. It may be encouraging to turn to a more successful example of the model in operation.

'Self-Interest and Common Good': the German Experience

The turbulent German historical experience has shaped the whole society somewhat according to the model of political economy described here. Business, politics and the enabling state interact in a fashion that has produced extraordinary results. Not least in this ensemble is the strong sense of local belonging. It has been suggested that for some centuries no German aged fifty has ever lived in the same country he or she was born in. But such a person may well have lived those fifty years in recognisably the same Länd, and has, Protestant or Catholic, been associated with the same regional Church. So the federal system has grown out of the lived experience of the people. This is of immense value in enabling taxes to be raised cheerfully—one of the main Bacon criteria—because they don't move far to be spent. Gray has an excellent summary of the German variant on the European model of political economy, with an interesting note that the Germans find the source of this version of the corporate state in Adam Smith.[23]

It is tedious to recount the coherence that has been established between business and workforce, between industrial requirements and training opportunities, between health care needs and provision. Unification and prolonged recession have naturally put it all under some strain, and this has concentrated the mind of the German Evangelical Church (EKD). This concentration of thought about what is going on in Germany now has resulted in an official document *Common Good and Self-Interest*.[24] This document looks seriously at the whole of society in a way that explicitly relates the elements of business, politics and the enabling state.

The document provides a plain description of the way the world works. The EKD start with the advantage that they have a well-established name for the model of political economy outlined above

—the social market economy. Its nature is briefly and lyrically described:

> The social market economy is not a rigid model but a dynamic process. It emanates from the lessons of history, and is geared to the flexibility of the market economy and to the discharge of new social duties. The social market economy is not a closed ideological system; it is open to different schools of thought and combines traditional elements of European liberalism, socialism and the Ecumenical Christian social movement. This is why the social market economy has proved itself as a model for integration and compromise in the sphere of economic activity, political responsibility and social commitment.[25]

On this holy mountain, the wolf truly lies down with the goat, and the lettuce is not consumed. The elements of the social order are described thus:

> The pure market economy components of economic life.

> The state framework and socio-cultural conditions into which the market economy processes are introduced and which must be taken due account of by market participants.

> State intervention in the economic process, where and when the market mechanism fails.

> The combination of the social with the economic, of social success with economic success.[26]

The document then goes on to ask some hard questions about social responsibility in German society. It is especially useful in exposing the false alternatives posed between socialism and capitalism, between economy and ecology.[27] It ridicules the 'Kick Ass' School of Business Ethics.[28] It takes a critical view of environmental responsibility. All this stands up very well because it is working from a model that does not reify, deify or diabolise the market.

The document also talks at length about Christian social responsibility in the world context. But this raises a set of problems which EKD has not properly thought out, as will be suggested below.

The Church in Civil Society

It is useful at this point to quote a passage from Bishop Martin Kruse's Introduction to the EKD document.

> The Council hopes that this memorandum will be the cause of intensive discussion at many levels—in local churches as well as in the realm of political responsibility, with representatives of industry and trade unions, with those who support and those who are critical of the social market economy.[29]

Here the Church is seeking to promote discussion, where interested parties pay serious attention to what makes our society work, and how it might best be understood and shaped for the common good. And this capacity for public reflection is a crucial part of the system's working. It has been suggested above that the institutional ensemble can work badly. It never works worse than when the managers of each institution act as if they were its proprietors, working chiefly to defend its interests against the other institutions—or even worse, when the institutions conspire together against the public. It is not enough to answer that this is a problem for the political institutions; they are as humanly frail as the rest, and need themselves to be engaged in continuous, affirmative but persistent discussion.

This is not to imagine that there is some substantive public which is separate from the institutions—a large part of the concerned public is engaged in business, politics or the enabling state. But there needs to be a sense in which institutional people lay aside their interests and seek some understanding of what it is all about. There needs to be some civil space in which this discussion takes place; the model needs another element if it is to be properly self-critical, and self-renewing. It is convenient to see in this continuous forum an important feature of *civil society*—indeed that area of civil society which it is the business of the Church consciously to occupy.

So now the model is complete, and perhaps we have discovered not only the proper subject of Christian social concern, but also its true location. It has been suggested that the Church mistakes its target when it addresses from a vaguely and implicitly Leftish standpoint the merits and shortcomings of 'capitalism'. There is, rather, a whole ensemble of institutions whose interaction is involved at every point of the social process, and criticism must be made in full awareness of this. But it would also be helpful if the Church were more conscious of the location from which it speaks. The Church is certainly a complex institution with a variety of theological and ecclesial traditions; but it is also a complex of interacting and conflicting lay vocations, all engaged in the life of a wider society. We have to find the nerve to let all this experience count, no matter how much it seems to complicate the issue. For instance, the official, clerical Church is tempted to speak up for the enabling state in the face of rapacious capitalism, ignoring our Tory voters who think with John Gray that the enabling state is a bit of a racket.

The renewing debate in civil society can obviously take place only if participants lay aside their vested interests and abandon their occupational postures. The Church also has interests to lay aside, and attitudes to abandon. It's worth doing. For instance, the question has been asked by Jacques Delors: 'Where is the heart and soul of Europe?' If anywhere, it is in this civil space where our common life is reflected on, prayed for, and where the future is imagined. This is the marketplace of our future belonging, where a myriad small stalls are set out, and what works best gets tested. It is also the point from which we best learn to pray for the whole. It may even be said that here the human republic is imagined, with restraint and humility, as the Republic of God.

This may sound fine. But a social order which is in any real sense open to civil society needs to grant minimum conditions of access. Here some phrases of Euro jargon are useful. First, *subsidiarity*. If institutions are geographically remote, they may be splendid, but splendidly inaccessible. Decision-making really must be taken at the level closest to the place where they take effect. Such subsidiarity must not be heavily conditional and contingent. People will only take seriously a local order which has a strong sense of *givenness*. If you are to appropriate the local, it must be yours, inviolably, and over time. The British case is especially illustrative of this problem. Not only is authority removed from the local, but that centralising authority has always regarded the local as its *tabula rasa*. In sharp contrast to the German experience, an historical series of fifty year old Britons has always lived in the same Britain they were born in— unless Irish. This has been roughly true for three and a half centuries. But a current such Briton has probably lived in at least three local polities, with another to come soon. civil society is not best nurtured in a revolving door.

A proper subsidiarity might also renew the capacity and morale of the local bureaucracy. It need not be only in the market system that actors are engrossed in achieving goals, seeking useful innovations, careful of valued customers.

Second, *transparency*. The private company and the public concern are closed to the British subject, as is Westminster, Whitehall and the Town Hall. It's true that Parliament is now televised, but if you sit in the aptly-named Stranger's Gallery and attempt to take notes, you'll be stopped. The business of local health administration is now becoming firmly closed to the public that it is supposed to serve. As Bacon might have said, the funding crisis of the British enabling state will become the sharper if consultation becomes increasingly partial. It is also a very odd polity indeed where the term 'British Citizen' has meaning only in the context of immigration control. The closed nature of British public culture might be a prime concern of the Church in Civil Society, rather than the misdeeds of the market.

There is enough here to engage the conscience and resources of the Church for some time to come. But we have discussed only the republic that is taking shape among the states of the European Community, as they shuffle, perhaps, towards something like a single polity. All the Christian authors mentioned earlier above soon begin to talk about the problems of capitalism in the world community. The framework described above has serious implications for the customary official Christian view of the world.

The Global Illusion

The problem is profound, but simply set out. Christians have a clear ideal of a global common good, but there is no structure that remotely embodies a common citizenship, a universal human republic. The Church tends to identify international capital as the essential part of the problem; but so deep is the problem that international capital may in fact be as much of a solution as is possible. In what has been said above, the bourgeois republic may be as good a place in which to be virtuous as history has ever offered; but in its nature it is deeply inimical to the universalisation of that potential for virtue. Such a suggestion has an overtone of the truly tragic, and needs explaining.

Fernand Braudel and others have shown us that the world economy is nothing new. But the tendrils of world trade formerly operated in spite of, rather than in concert with, the polities across which they operated. Even more strikingly, the medieval Muslim travelling theologian, Ibn Batuta, reveals rather inadvertently the nature of a world economy. He travelled from his Moroccan homeland on the Atlantic to Pacific China along paths created by Islamic traders, in whose business he took virtually no interest; but he offers a laconic, clerical swipe at the market, as he speaks of a particularly arid desert:

> One year the pilgrims suffered terribly here from the samoom-wind; the water supplies dried up and the price of a single drink rose to a thousand dinars; but both seller and buyer perished.[30]

The theocratic principalities of this Muslim world occupied a moral space somewhat above that of the humble traders. Here there may be a humane society, but no human republic.

With the accession of the trading nation, first of all Bacon's Dutch, the world changes decisively. We now have societies organised self-consciously around trade, then around democratic politics, then around the enabling state. The existence of such polities, admittedly hugely involved in the control of international capital, requires our attention.

The model of political economy offered above has certain international implications. The states of Western Europe are *compulsory societies* of a sort conceivable only by the great dictators. The power to tax, plan, reorganise is enormous and ubiquitous, and possible only because it is based on some kind of consent. The great intensity of this kind of relationship must be contrasted with the sparser environment of international relationships, including world trade. The world of the single human republic is almost all-consuming, while that of international relations is voluntary and tentative. The single polity is like a black hole in the void of interstellar space.

This *particularity* of modern industrial states is vividly revealed by Ernest Gellner:

> An overwhelming part of political authority has been concentrated in the hands of one kind of institution, a reasonably large and well-centralised state. In general, each state presides over, maintains, and is identified with, one kind of culture, one style of communication, which prevails within its borders and is dependent for its perpetuation on a centralised educational system supervised by and often actually run by the state in question, which monopolises legitimate culture almost as much as it does legitimate violence, or perhaps more so.[31]

There are currently three major examples of this total state. Two are the United States and Japan. The third is either Germany or the European Community. It should be noted that for Gellner, culture is the leading factor in the formation and maintenance of statehood; economics follows in the baggage train. This is not the 'culture' of complacent windbaggery, but the clearly defined outcome of the central function of the enabling state; a common education, almost inevitably based on a single language in each system. This judgment points up sharply the improbability of a Federal European Republic.

The case of the European Community is somewhat crucial. For here is an attempt to create something like a new polity, a federation of bourgeois republics, increasingly modelled on the social market economy. But it seems to have been conceded among the member states that the Community's objectives cannot be achieved without something like the level of compulsion that applies in each member state. It is increasingly clear that the degree of consent necessary to sustain such compulsion is not possible on a Community-wide basis. How much less is it likely that world harmony based on international agreement can be achieved without a mind-boggling level of such compulsion. It is ironic if what is essentially a European model of political economy is unworkable within a united European polity, but no more than this; the quality of the model does not depend essentially on its capacity to cross cultural divides that may be unbridgeable. A decreasing number of people want to find out the hard way whether close European union has a Swiss or a Yugoslavian future.

So, no matter how Europe sorts itself out, the 21st Century is unlikely to be chiefly characterised by an increasing internationalism, with the forces of good locked in combat with the powers of global capital, on the side of justice, peace and the integrity of creation. The 21st Century will more likely be marked by the rise of two vast bourgeois republics in China and India; possibly a third if Russia can get its baggage train sorted out; and whoever else can arrange consent for this kind of compulsory society. But the pattern for the bulk of the Eurasian landmass will not simply be that of its tiny northwest corner. The new republics will no doubt be at least as different as Japan and the United States. They seem likely to be formed on the basis of the market economy, increasingly free politics and the enabling state, with space in civil society to test new forms of relation between these elements.

All this suggests that the Church should abandon its global illusion, that sentimental vision of a readily achievable world order, frustrated only by the machinations of the powerful. International agreement is desirable and urgent in a number of crucial areas; but this agreement will be reached between highly discrete states; and this separateness is likely to intensify rather than to diminish.

The standard ecclesiastical global vision seems at first sight to be terribly parochial. Most of the world's poor people live in a small number of huge states within the Eurasian landmass, notably India, China and the former Soviet Union. But the church tends continually to illustrate its case with reference to Africa and Latin America. It is certainly true that the poverty of these regions is intractable in very special ways; but it is also true that these are the missionary heartlands of the past four centuries. So that when we talk globally, we tend not simply to be contemplating the future of the world, but also reflecting on the history of the Church. Botswana and El Salvador are certainly interesting places; but interesting times too are occurring between the Gulf of Finland and the Gulf of Tonkin, and on a somewhat larger scale. Once again, our model of international relations is wrong, as is our model of political economy. Moreover, the two errors are interlinked, and compound one another.

This said, however, the Church has a crucial witness to make in the cause of those countries closest to its heart. Such a witness will inconveniently recall the dreadful sufferings inflicted upon the world as a result of the European urge to empire. It can of course be argued that European imperialism was the curse of the human republic, and that this evil perished, along with millions of Europeans, in the single cataclysm that began in 1914 and ended (let us say) in 1945. From this perspective, imperial Europe suffered as terribly as any from its own dominating impulses. Nonetheless, much of Africa and Latin America have been shaped by external historical forces that have denied them the capacity to develop their own versions of the human republic. The collapse of Leninist power in the world leaves the Church with a distinctive vocation in this desperate area; the vocation of Desmond Tutu, of Oscar Romero. But the Church must not persuade itself that these societies are the whole of the poor world; and must grasp the truth that the market helps poor people.

Christian Vocation in the Human Republic

The European model of political economy described above may claim to be as good a framework for the exercise of public virtue that the world has yet devised, and that markedly different but recognisably similar versions of this model may shape the development of world society for the foreseeable future.

The Church seems to have a persistent tendency to resist one element of this model, the market; indeed, to isolate it from the whole for faint praise or thoroughgoing damns. Some features of this tendency need examination.

First, the Church has a powerful instinct to allocate. This owes something to the monarchic nature of its texts; much of the Old Testament is phrased interims of judgment upon kingly rule; God is also fairly monarchic. So there is an instinctive tendency to desire some kind of Command Economy, with the implication that the command can somehow be made divine. Hence the attachment in history to theories of just wage and just price.

This tendency inclines the tradition to fix Jesus' notions of the Kingdom of God in a particular dogmatic frame. Our Lord's many and mystifying sayings about the Kingdom tend to be regarded as a desire for an egalitarian monarchy. But the Kingdom might better be regarded as rather more like the human republic; nobody absolutely in charge, open to the future, free but under obedience, canny about human failings, idealistic about human possibilities, a goodish place to be virtuous in. Indeed, our Lord's homely illustrations from the world of buying and selling confirm the normality— and arguably the normative nature—of that world.

Second, the ascetic tradition. At last we come to the second part of our text: Bacon's 'Prosperity is the blessing of the Old Testament, adversity is the blessing of the New'.

The validity of the Christian ascetic tradition can be argued endlessly; one opinion might see it as central to the teaching of Jesus; another will see it much more in the tradition of John the Baptist, and that one major purpose of the Luke's Gospel is to make this point. But this ascetic view is not just critical of the market; it is critical of the whole ensemble. It is not about fairness, it is about frugality. If it points out the failings of prosperity, it can do so only in order to condemn the notion, not to adjust it.

The converse of Bacon's proposition makes his argument sharply ironic. Thus adversity is a problem for the Old Testament; Job's trials would be welcomed by a serious Christian ascetic. And it follows that prosperity is a problem for the New. But Max Weber seems to be right in suggesting that some forms of Christianity carry in them a wealth-creating quality. The Christian condition then becomes even more interesting; some Christians are always creating more wealth for the others to feel guilty about. There is a kind of divine equilibrium here, and perhaps the main fund-raising strategy of the churches down the ages. There is an almost alchemical wonder to the scheme: 'This is the famous stone that turneth guilt to gold'. There is an irony here that adds deeply to the amusement and to the strength of vocation of aware ascetics; they know that there's a very odd game going on.

But the truly ascetic vocation is voluntary. Those who choose it seek a personal and communal solution, in the cave and in the monastery. To treat the whole world as a failed holy order is deeply mistaken; the ethic of the monastery made universal and compulsory ends in the Gulag.

The monarchic and ascetic traditions in the Church are, it can be argued, a hindrance to a proper understanding of how the world works, and therefore what is possible in it. Within these traditions lies a sensibility that creates a moral distance from the human republic, and which tends to treat that world with a kind of disdain. There is, in short, a kind of spiritual snobbery, a false sense of nobility. It is, of course, quite possible to break out of this sensibility, to affirm the human republic and its real achievements; then the deep resources of the Christian tradition come into their own, and exercise a liberating power.

The tradition has the power to liberate the human republic from its great curse—its pervasive sense of self-sufficiency, its tendency to turn everything into a constructive project, including belief. But the Christian tradition that seems so out of tune with the modern world has the ability to introduce ambiguity, to break down our illusion of being in charge. The Christian image of God as ruler of all is not merely archaic. The Almighty is the one whom we come before without our abilities, and it here that we are no longer citizen but subject. Indeed, it may be a paradox of citizenship that it is only sustainable where the burgher is this subject, at a point at which the human republic becomes God's kingdom; the point where imagination catches a vision of transformation that goes beyond our schemes for improvement.

Closely allied to this is the broader insight of the ascetic tradition. It may be virtually impossible to affirm the prosperity of bourgeois society without being totally immersed in its possibilities. This is especially the case when the sensibility of consumerism is identified as *the liberation of human desire*. It is bad that we consume the material universe so voraciously, but we increasingly consume each other; we live less with one another, more off one another, as the Italian proverb predicts.

As Simon Schama and others have argued, the notion of the burgher, the citizen, rather than the bourgeois 'homo oeconomicus', has some connection with the sense of vocation that characterises the ascetic tradition; but of calling into rather than out of the world. Living out such a calling can be confusing and ambiguous, as it seeks to cope with all the experience that life hurls around. The Methodist Church, a creature both of the Holy Spirit and of commercial and industrial England, has been perhaps the most 'burger-lich' of all the British Christian communities. It has in its texts an interesting response to the contradictions of finding a Christian vocation in the market place. Thus the words of the Methodist Covenant:

> Put me to what you will, rank me with whom you will; put me to doing, put me to suffering; let me be employed for you or laid aside for you, exalted for you or brought low for you; let me be full, let me be empty; let me have all things, let me have nothing...

In such a sensibility, the insights of the ascetic tradition are carried forward into a world dominated by chance and change, and are enabled to survive outside the confines of an enclosed religious style. Some such sense of vocation is essential to the maintenance of any order, and especially one so complex, demanding and power-laden as the human republic. The instinct of the Church is fundamentally right, however, in seeing the market as the great potential solvent of vocation. There is, after all, a certain anxiety, a bravado, about the Methodist assertion of vocation in a very chancy world. This is why it so crucial a part of the calling of the Church to explore what the best political context for the market might be.

The Church has to be clear about the difficulty of vocation in so uncertain a world. But it must not give the impression that there is some noble, timeless, risk-free alternative at its disposal. The Church must be free to arouse in itself and the world a vision of transformation; but this most not lead it to despise the machinery of improvement. The human republic is not the Kingdom of God, but it does have a persuasive claim to be affirmed as a demanding and congenial setting for the Christian vocation. It may even so influence the Christian vision of transformation that the Church may begin to ponder what the Republic of God might be like—but perhaps not yet.

Notes

1   Bacon, F., *The Essays, 1626*, London: Penguin, 1985, p. 99.

2   *Ibid.*, p. 75.

3   John Paul II, *Centesimus Annus*, London: Catholic Truth Society, 1991.

4   Harries, R., *Is There A Gospel For The Rich?*, London: Mowbray, 1992.

5   Preston, R.C., *Religion and the Ambiguities of Capitalism*, London: SCM Press, 1991.

6   Hay, D., *Economics Today*, Leiceister: Apollos, 1989.

7   Gray, J., *The Moral Foundations of Market Institutions*, London: IEA Health and Welfare Unit, 1992.

8   Braudel, F., *Civilization & Capitalism*, vol. I-III, London: Collins, 1981.

9   Schama, S., *The Embarrassment of Riches: An Interpretation of Dutch Culture in the Golden Age*, London; Collins, 1987, p. 7.

110

10 Novak, M. *The Spirit of Democratic Capitalism*, London: IEA Health and Welfare Unit, 1991.

11 Braudel, F., *op. cit.*, vol. I, pp. 31-51.

12 Himmelfarb, G., *The Idea of Poverty*, London: Faber, 1985.

13 Smith, A., *An Inquiry into the Nature and Causes of the Wealth of Nations*, Oxford: Oxford University Press, 1976, pp. 688-89.

14 *Ibid.*, p. 782.

15 Gray, J., *op. cit.*, p. 75.

16 Marquand, D., *The Unprincipled Society*, London: Cape, 1988.

17 *Ibid.*, p. 241.

18 *Inequalities in Health*, London: DHSS, 1980.

19 Archbishop of Canterbury's Commission on Urban Priority Areas, *Faith in the City*, London: Church Publishing House, 1985.

20 Goodin, R. and Le Grand, J., *Not Only the Poor*, London: Allen & Unwin, 1987.

21 George, P., *No Mean City*, Peterborough: Methodist Publishing House, 1989.

22 Gray, J., *op. cit.*, p. 87.

23 *Ibid.*, pp. 81-84.

24 EKD (Evangelische Kirche in Deutschland), *Common Good and Self Interest*, Hannover, Germany: EKD, 1992.

25 *Ibid.*, p. 16.

26 *Ibid.*, p. 17.

27 *Ibid.*, pp. 59-61.

28 *Ibid.*, p. 18.

29 *Ibid.*, p. 4.

30 Ibn Batuta, M., *Travels in Asia and Africa 1325-1354*, London: Routledge & Kegan Paul, 1984, p. 73.

31 Gellner, E., *Nations and Nationalism*, Oxford: Blackwell, 1984, p. 140.

Beyond Competition

Geoff Moore

There is an interesting dichotomy between the views of economists and those of businessmen on the subject of competition. Economists view competition as an essential element of a market system; something to be encouraged if scarce resources are to be used in the most efficient manner. Businessmen, on the other hand, view competition as something to be avoided or defeated—almost as though it were an unfortunate outcome of a market system. Since most western/northern economists and businessmen are committed to capitalism, this dichotomy might at first sight seem strange; one would think that they were on the same side. How, then, does this dichotomy come about?

Competition arises from self-interest, which is the basic motivating force behind our economic system. Given the existence of scarce resources, at least for each persons desired level of material well-being, (and in contrast to the Biblical understanding of the world as a place of abundance), self-interest leads to rivalry for those scarce resources. Hence competition, whether on an individual basis or on the collective basis of the business organisation, is born. (It is interesting to note in passing that we are encouraged to subjugate our self-interest—the basic motivating force—to cooperate with others within the business organisation, in order to compete more effectively with those outside the organisation. This gives rise to a kind of schizophrenia, to which we will return.)

The economist's view of competition, then, can be summed up succinctly in the words of T.E.Utley:

> The result of economic competition, conducted within the framework of fair and settled law, will be that everyone will end up in the job that he

is best fitted to do, and that the economic needs of the community will be precisely identified and swiftly and efficiently satisfied.[1]

This statement clearly has echoes of Adam Smith's 'employment which is most advantageous to society'[2] and bears out the social case for capitalism since the society's or the community's needs are believed to be met most efficiently through this process. The economic 'ideals' of consumer sovereignty, perfect competition and profit maximisation hence find their social justification.

What, then, is the businessman's view of competition? The businessman's view is that everyone is against him, for, following Porter's analysis 'customers, suppliers, potential entrants and substitute products are all competitors' in addition to the 'established combatants in a particular industry'.[3] Thus competition is derived from five directions, not one, and it is the corporate strategist's goal to 'find a position in the industry where his or her company can best defend itself against these forces or can influence them in its favour'.[4] Competitive rivalry—the jockeying for position among the current competitors—is the most obvious of these forces. In marketing terms the market is only so big and the efforts of each 'player', therefore, have to be directed towards obtaining market share, at the expense of the other 'players'.

But competition is also rife between suppliers and buyers. Any particular firm will constantly seek to obtain the best deal from its suppliers; the lowest price for the highest quality. And the extent of its power over its suppliers will determine how effectively it achieves its aim. Thus, Marks and Spencer will obtain a better deal from a vegetable wholesaler than a local chain of general dealers which stocks a limited range and requires small quantities. Supplier power, or lack of it, is another competitive force which can affect the profit potential of an industry.

Supplier power is, of course, a two-edged sword, for firms not only attempt to obtain the best deal from their suppliers but find their customers doing the same to them. Buyer power—the ability of customers to dictate price/quality parameters—is the third competitive force.

Substitute products (margarine replacing butter, for example) can have a devastating effect on an industry. But more frequently the effect is less disastrous, while nonetheless imposing price/performance constraints as firms seek to persuade customers to remain loyal to their product.

Finally, the threat of new entrants to an industry, where this is credible, again reduces the profit potential of the industry because of the need to defend the position of the firm—by being prepared to cut prices or increase marketing or Research and Development expenditures, for example.

When viewed in the light of this analysis, the economist's desire to encourage competition, or at least to aim towards the ideal of a perfectly competitive market, involves seeking a market where the competitive forces are evenly balanced: strong rivalry between current competitors; comparably strong suppliers and customers; sufficient threat of substitutes and new entrants. And the more competitors in the market, the more likely this state of affairs is to arise.

From the businessman's point of view, such a market is a nightmare! A market in which there is nowhere to hide, in which no force is weak and can be exploited, is a market with little or no profit potential. Thus Porter's prescriptions, accepting that no such market exists in practice, emphasise the objectives of avoiding or defeating the forces ranged against it.

Thus 'positioning the company' involves 'building defences against the competitive forces or...finding positions in the industry where the forces are weakest'.[5] An interesting example of this is the current tendency, advocated by contemporary management gurus[6] of forging links with suppliers. This at least controls this particular competitive force, while also being a further example of the 'co-operate in order to compete' syndrome noted above.

'Influencing the balance' is an offensive strategy which seeks to alter the causes of the competitive forces. Forward integration (taking over or competing with your customers) is an example of this and is practised by many firms. Thus Virgin moved from a firm with a record label to high street mega-stores before selling out to EMI.

Porter's third prescription—exploiting industry change—is a reactive approach which seeks to adapt to new developments in an industry by taking advantage of them. Small brewers have found the 1989 Monopolies and Mergers' Commission ruling limiting the number of pubs a brewer can own, an opportunity to expand as larger brewers were forced to sell off pubs.

Businessmen, then, seek continually to gain 'competitive advantage', to steal a march, to take advantage of weaknesses in the competitive forces ranged against them. The ideal position for a business might well be in a niche which lasts or a monopoly which cannot be broken.

One corollary of this is that those governments which, like economists, believe in competition, act to prevent the distortions of the market which business, if left to its own devices, would bring about. So, for example, regulators for privatised public utilities, the Monopolies and Mergers' Commission and lower tax burdens for smaller firms are all ways in which the Government in the UK seeks to redress the balance and ensure healthy, if not perfect, competition.

One problem is that such governments often find it difficult to go far enough in their promotion of competition. Governments cannot force markets to become more highly competitive by advantaging the weak and penalising the strong—to do so would be to alienate the strong (often their allies) and to engage in the exact opposite of the free market they wish to create. Over-involvement soon becomes central direction.

Thus we arrive at a situation where traces of any kind of perfect market are hard to find. Sympathetic economists such as Todaro admit as much: 'Consumers are rarely sovereign about anything, let alone with regard to questions of what goods and services are to be produced, in what quantities and for whom. Producers, whether private or public, have great power in determining market prices and quantities to be sold. The ideal of competition is often just that: an 'ideal' with little relation to reality. Finally the so-called invisible hand often acts not to promote the general welfare of all but to lift up those who are already well-off while pushing down that vast majority of the population which is striving to free itself from poverty, malnutrition and illiteracy'.[7]

This is a damning indictment of the free market which begins to link together the flaws in a market system with the plight of many in the Third World. This may seem a rather large step, but when we consider that Third World producers often have little 'supplier' power, may be disadvantaged by tariff or quota trade barriers, and may find their product subject to speculation on some futures market,[8] it is not difficult to see that Porter's analysis of competitive forces has particular application to Third World-First World trade. (These market flaws, however, are equally in evidence within developed countries, where unemployment and poverty—exclusion from the market itself—are common features of life for a significant minority.)

Todaro's thesis is supported by Vallely[9] who identifies seven flaws in the market system and offers a four stage response: relief based on charitable giving; development which is aimed at longer term improvements in material conditions; justice, which recognises that the poor do not exist in poverty simply because of the size of the problem, but are actually kept in poverty by the very structures of international trade and finance; and empowerment, in which the role of the First World must be to enable the people of the Third World to take control of their own lives. We will return to this analysis below.

Leaving aside aid for immediate relief, the contemporary solutions to these problems seem either to distort the market or open up companies and countries to the full blast of free-market economics. We have already observed how governments attempt to encourage competition by, for example, keeping the tax burden low for smaller firms. On an international scale, trade protectionism by the imposition of tariffs or quotas or the giving of subsidies is designed to fend off foreign competition and protect infant or ailing industries. These actions inevitably distort the market. At the opposite extreme, export-promotion strategies[10] and IMF austerity packages are designed to open up companies and nations to the free market. Thus neither route finds a path through the market system which harnesses the positive side of the market (its ability to match demand and supply reasonably accurately and with relatively little waste, and its giving of independence and respect to individuals by allowing them to exercise choice), while avoiding the worst effects already identified.

God and the Market Place

So does Christianity have anything to offer to this situation where there is apparently no middle road? And if it does, are there practical examples to which we can point? And if so, do these practical examples have any chance of success in a secular world? It is to these questions that we now turn.

This is not the place (and nor is the author the person) to carry out a detailed analysis of the understanding of the market which Biblical and Christian historical tradition hands down to us. But a few points are necessary in order to link the preceding analysis with some practical solutions.

From Biblical tradition three important aspects emerge: first that God is a God of justice; second that the flaws inherent in an economic free-for-all are recognised and remedies provided; and third (and more arguably) that the approach to economics is laissez-faire, but subject to these remedies.

'According to Biblical testimony, God enters history and reveals himself, in that God frees the Hebrews who were marginalised and oppressed by the advanced imperial civilisations (Exodus 3). This is the way God's justice acts through the whole Biblical history.

God's justice consists in saving the poor, the weak, the oppressed, where necessary by overcoming the strong, the oppressor'.[11] Thus we find verses such as Amos 5:24 'But let justice roll down like waters, and righteousness like an ever-flowing stream' [RSV] and Micah 6:8 'He has showed you O man what is good; and what does the Lord require of you, but to do justice, and to love kindness and to walk humbly with your God?' [RSV]

God's justice extends into the economic sphere. Thus, for example, usury, at least among the people of Israel, was condemned (Exodus 22:25). But what is of particular interest in the context of the previous discussion are the rules for the Sabbath Year and the Jubilee. In the Sabbath Year 'you must cancel debts... Every creditor shall cancel the loan he has made to his fellow Israelite' (Deut. 15:1,2) [NIV]. Not only this, but all slaves were to be set free—and sent out with a liberal helping of sheep, grain and wine (Deut 15:12-14)! At the Jubilee these principles seem to be extended: 'And you shall hallow the fiftieth year, and proclaim liberty throughout the land to all its inhabitants; it shall be a jubilee for you, when each of you shall return to his property and each of you shall return to his family' (Lev 25:10) [RSV].

The implications from these early Biblical times is that economic relations had to be conducted in an honest and just way, but also in a way which allowed, to a certain extent, winners and losers. Those who lost would become indebted or, at worst, enslaved to those who won. This reflects the laissez-faire attitude to economic relations mentioned above. But inherent in the system was a recognition that it would not take long for the 'level playing field' to start to slope quite distinctly. Hence the Sabbath Year and the Jubilee provided not only a way out of indebtedness and slavery for the individual, but also a means of restoring the level playing field. In addition, such a system would control avarice because the incentive of long-term gain was removed. From the pure economist's viewpoint, this might sound like a good idea; the distortions of the market are ironed out every so often and perfect competition is restored!

Whether or not the Sabbath Year and the Jubilee were ever put into practice, the nature of divine revelation is such that these concepts need to be taken seriously. The 'laissez-faire coupled with powerful remedies' approach seems to have much to say to our present situation.

Two concepts which developed in the Reformation thinking in this area seem to relate back to this Biblical basis. Once it was generally agreed that interest could be charged on loans, there arose the issue of what was a reasonable rate of interest. Here was an opportunity for gain by those who had over those who had not. But the Church, in the form of John Calvin, was quite convinced that the rate should not exceed a legal maximum, and indeed 'a Geneva Church Ordinance in 1541 allowed interest of 5 per cent, raising it to 6.7 per cent in 1557'.[12] While this has no obvious links with the Sabbath Year or Jubilee, it could be argued that such a ruling was designed to keep the playing field reasonably level rather than restore it at intervals, and so stemmed from the same concern for economic justice.

Similarly the concept of the just price—where the level of profit corresponds to 'the time and trouble incurred, and the ordinary need for a livelihood'[13]—was designed to set a limit on the possibilities of gain whether achieved through economic power or by taking advantage of ignorance. Again, the effect would be to keep the playing field reasonably level by ensuring that no advantages were taken in the supplier-buyer relationship.

While neither of these concepts has lasted—in the seventeenth century the just price was considered by the Schoolmen to be the market price—they nonetheless hold out some practical means by which the flaws in the market system might be remedied. Are there, then, practical examples to which we can point, where these concepts are being employed today?

Practical Examples

Since the conference was held in Newcastle upon Tyne, it seems appropriate to consider two examples one of which, Traidcraft plc, began in Newcastle, and the other of which, Shared Interest Society Ltd, is based there.

Traidcraft, which is now located a few miles south west of Newcastle, began in 1979 as an importer of mainly craft goods from Third World countries. In the thirteen years since then it has grown rapidly, having today a turnover approaching £6m and a range of goods which includes tea, coffee, wholefoods, clothing, jewellery and recycled paper as well as the craft goods with which it began. It sells through three main channels—an army of 'voluntary representatives' who purchase goods at a discount and sell them through home-meetings, stalls and direct contact with customers; a mail order catalogue; and shops, a few of which it owns itself.

In its objectives the company states that 'Traidcraft aims to expand and establish trading systems which are more just and which express the principles of love and justice fundamental to the Christian faith. Its objectives arise from a commitment to practical service and partnership for change, which puts people before profit'.[14]

Expanding on this mission statement, the objectives go on to say that the distinctive trading system which Traidcraft aims to contribute to 'will be a system based on service, equity and justice drawing its driving force from those values applied in love' and that it will 'regard the existence of gross material inequities between peoples, where some are without the basic means to enjoy health, security and opportunity for personal fulfilment and development, as a condition to be remedied through the economic system and not perpetuated by it'.[15]

Within its purchasing policy several of these principles are expanded upon: 'Traidcraft has always emphasised in its trading policy its commitment to: paying fair prices to producers; helping with working capital by making advanced payments with purchase orders where appropriate; not switching suppliers simply to obtain more competitive price or delivery terms; a preference for products where the maximum value is added locally'.[16]

Here, then, is a company attempting to work within the present economic system, but doing so on a distinctly different basis. There is considerable emphasis on justice, together with means for correcting the flaws of the market system. The concept of the just price is evident if not explicit. In terms of Vallely's four stages in development mentioned above, Traidcraft is clearly working at the third and fourth levels of justice and empowerment.

Since Traidcraft is deliberately operating someway towards the bottom of a playing field which slopes fairly steeply, it is not surprising that it has had difficulties. The company had an accumulated deficit in its profit and loss account of £158,000 in 1991. It has survived and grown largely through a policy of paying relatively low (but just?) wages, and with the assistance of a committed shareholding base of around £2m which has not seen a dividend since 1986.

The second example is an organisation which, in a way, grew out of Traidcraft's work, though it is now entirely separate. One of the needs which companies such as Traidcraft had identified was for investment finance for companies in the Third World. It is often difficult for companies in Third World countries to raise investment finance at all, or to do so at reasonable rates of interest. Consequently, opportunities to expand or export are curtailed. Traidcraft, as we have seen, operates a policy of providing cash advances to those producer groups which would be otherwise unable to accept an order for want of working capital to purchase raw materials. While this is a good way of assisting growth, the resources of companies like Traidcraft are limited, and such up-front financing inevitably eats in to margins which are already tight.

The need, then, for some form of investment vehicle for channelling funds into Third World, and other, companies was apparent. Indeed, Traidcraft had approached the Bank of England about the possibility of obtaining banking status back in 1982, but had been categorically discouraged.

Shared Interest Society Ltd., incorporated under the Industrial and Provident Society Act 1965, was established in April 1990 to 'carry on the business of providing financial services, especially for production and trade, in a manner which reflects the principles of love, justice and stewardship which are fundamental to the faith of the Christian Church and are accepted by many other people of goodwill and compassion and in order to promote wholesome, dignified and sustainable employment for the benefit of people in need in any part of the world, particularly in poor countries'.[17]

In many respects the Society resembles a Building Society share account: shareholders are members of the Society and entitled to vote at AGMs; the minimum shareholding is £250 and the maximum £10,000; shares carry the risk of loss, are repayable on demand and receive interest (before tax) at a variable rate; there are no management charges or fees. The differences from a Building Society account lie in the high minimum amount, the relatively low interest rate (currently 2.5 per cent), the relatively high risk and, of course, the objects behind the organisation.

The choice of name—Shared Interest—reflects some of these differences. It deliberately invokes the use of both 'share' and 'interest' as financial terms appropriate to the type of organisation, while clearly giving the message that the return will be less than the commercial rate because of the principle of sharing with those who are recipients of the investment funds.

The primary method of investment in the Third World is through the Ecumenical Development Co-operative Society (EDCS). This is a Dutch-based organisation which is the result of an initiative by the World Council of Churches. It was set up in 1975 as a response to the imbalance of wealth in the world, the intention being that it would be a commercially viable vehicle through which the churches could invest part of their considerable endowment funds with the poor of the Third World. However, the churches as institutions have been content to follow rather than lead, and it has been left to individuals, often via support associations established in a number of countries, to provide the funds.

With over £20m invested in it, most of its 10 staff being Third World-based Project Development Officers, and more than 100 projects behind it, EDCS can claim to be one of the most experienced organisations in investment in Third World companies at the grass-roots level. Consequently, Shared Interest decided to invest at least 50 per cent of its first £4m share capital in EDCS. In addition, Shared Interest has made loans to other First World organisations engaged in the relief of poverty through trade.

Like Traidcraft, Shared Interest is seeking to work within the present economic system, but in a distinctive way. Again the concept of the just price is evident and indeed the Industrial and Provident Societies Act imposes the condition that the interest payable should not exceed the 'minimum rate necessary...to obtain and retain the capital required to carry out the objects of the society'.[18] So far the Society has grown rapidly, reaching a share capital of around £2.5m, and showing a small surplus at the end of each of the first two trading periods.

God in the Marketplace

Sceptics would almost certainly argue that by deliberately altering the market price for the goods and services which they trade in—Traidcraft paying more and Shared Interest charging less—these two organisations are operating against the interests of society by distorting the competitive instinct—in Adam Smith's words, 'I have never known much good done by those who affected to trade for the public good'.[19] But the burden of proof should surely lie on the other side, with sceptics being asked to defend a market price which is so obviously distorted by the many factors identified earlier (to say nothing of shorter-term marketing strategies), and a market system which so clearly leaves many questions to do with justice unanswered.

Yet even if these sceptics fail to defend their position, the role of organisations like Traidcraft and Shared Interest seems likely to remain marginal at best. For, in the final analysis, it is not simply their calls for justice which motivate those involved, but the power of the love which seeks others' highest good rather than self-interest. A society with just economic relations, where love is the motivating and guiding force, is the ideal to which they aim. And within a secular society, where such a motivating force is seldom in evidence, the concepts of love and justice seem unlikely to capture the imagination of even a small minority of people. The minimal impact of the New Economic International Order movement, endorsed by the UN General Assembly in 1974, the Brandt

Report in 1979 and its successor, Common Crisis in 1983, all bear witness to this.

But perhaps there is one small ray of light on the horizon. For, as noted above, the idea that we have to cooperate in order to compete, seems to be increasingly understood. Cooperation within the organisation, cooperation between organisations and their suppliers and, at the next level, cooperation between competing organisations by forming joint ventures are all accepted business practice. Now clearly all of this is still with a view to gaining competitive advantage over those not involved with these links. And while the gulf between cooperating in order to compete, and cooperating in order to cooperate seems unbridgeable—and the consequent dangers of monopoly power very obvious—it would at least appear that the language is one which Christians and the secular world can agree on. As Vallely points out, 'Cooperation and not competition is the natural basis of the Christian approach'.[20]

Is there, perhaps, economic life beyond competition?

Notes

1 Utley, T.E., *Capitalism The Moral Case*, 1980.

2 Smith, Adam, Cannon, E. (ed), *An Inquiry into the Nature and Causes of the Wealth of Nations*, London: 1904.

3 Porter, M., 'How Competitive Forces Shape Strategy', *Harvard Business Review*, 1979.

4 Porter, M., *op. cit.*

5 *Ibid.*

6 See, for example, Peters, Tom, *Thriving on Chaos*, Macmillan, 1987.

7 Todaro, M.P., *Economics for a Developing World*, 3rd edition, Longman, 1992.

8 For a comprehensive analysis of this imbalance of power, see Vallely, P., *Bad Samaritans*, Hodder and Stoughton, 1990, Ch. 3.

9 *Ibid.*

10 See Torado, M.P., *op. cit.*, Ch. 22.

124

11 Duchrow, U., *The Witness of the Church in Contrast to the Ideologies of the Market Economy*, in the final report of the International Consultation organised by the West European Network on Work, Unemployment and the Churches, held at Evangelische Akademie, Mulheim/Ruhr, Germany, April 1988.

12 Preston, R., 'Is There a Christian Ethic of Finance?, in *Finance and Ethics*, Centre for Theology and Public Issues, 1987.

13 Samuelsson, Kurt, *Religion and Economic Action*, Heinemann, 1961.

14 Traidcraft Objectives, 1986.

15 *Ibid*.

16 Traidcraft purchasing policy, 1989.

17 Shared Interest Society Ltd., Rule 3.

18 Shared Interest Society., Rule 6.

19 Smith, Adam, *op. cit.*

20 Vallely, P., *op. cit.*

Some Reflections from the Perspective of Ministry in Secular Employment

Rev Dr James Francis

The marketplace is for so many, in varied participatory ways, a place of endeavour, creativity and fulfilment. Such a claim remains true despite the occasional manifestations of greed and dishonesty which can emerge (sometimes spectacularly) into public gaze, and despite the dangers of a competitiveness which can absorb too much of wider creative human potential. Nonetheless a sense of purposive living is for many (and perhaps for all of us even though it may be unacknowledged) bound up with the necessity of the marketplace.

It was the particular genius of Hebrew faith to bequeath to Christianity a vision of God Who is both in relation to and yet other than the world He has created. It is this paradox which may provide one of the best ways toward the rediscovery of the contribution of the Church's faith to the marketplace, especially for its significance in the work setting itself. That is to say the very relationship of God to His world, and His concern for it, is through an 'otherness' which reminds us that we as people can indeed discover our creativity in our work, but that creativity cannot and should not be exhausted by economic activity itself. Equally it is just this sense of the transcendent in the realisation not of 'wanting more' but of exploring more and more of who we are in sustainable and worthwhile endeavour which may more suitably translate issues of performance from 'productivity' (a mechanistic framework) to 'contribution' (a humane framework).

It is significant that normative Judaism expressed this awareness of God, as He who is both in relation to His world and yet other than His world, through the idea of 'creating' rather than 'conceiving'. (The latter would tend to 'divinise' the world, or to reduce the divine to a 'commonality of being' with the world.) In Hebrew perspective God is in relationship to His world precisely by being other than it, and it is this sense of transcendence which is implied in the belief that He created the world, or to put it another way, that the world is His 'handiwork'. This is important for our present discussion for two reasons—a) it demonstrates a particular way of holding belief and craftsmanship together (God could be described in Rabbinic thought as the true or ultimate Artisan/Craftsman), and b) it enables us to hold on to a sense of the transcendent which addresses the meaning and worth of work i.e. if God is 'more than' because He is 'other than' the world, we therefore are 'more than' what we produce, but we are able to express creativity precisely by being part of, and participant in, what we produce.

Don Cupitt makes the following relevant comment about technology in a theistic context:

> ...theism from the beginning employed imagery derived from technology, when it spoke of God as maker or creator of the world, rather than begetting it.... Anaximander's brilliant cosmological speculations owed something to seeing a potter's wheel, and steam from a boiling kettle condensing. Certainly his drum-shaped earth in stable equilibrium looks very like a lump of clay centred properly upon a wheel, and his account of the formation of the heavenly bodies reads as if he imagined a spinning mass throwing off a spiral of steam which condenses into orbiting drops. But Anaximander's contemporary in Israel, Jeremiah, also went down to learn from the potter (Jer.18.1ff). The difference is that Anaximander's attention was concentrated on the behaviour of the clay, Jeremiah's on the hands of the potter. The Israelites were interested in technology, and they did not suppose that its secrets had been stolen by man from the Gods. They did not oppose religion and technology: on the contrary, it could probably be shown that every trade and craft known to them at one time or another furnished imagery of theism—the

refiner's fire, the metal worker's forge, the irrigation of dry land, bleaching with fuller's earth, building, and working clay on the wheel.[1]

This quotation is instructive for the summary which it provides of two different ways by which belief is related to human activity. In the myth of Prometheus human creativity emerges as a kind of theft by which divine fire is stolen and, thus wrested from its divine origin, becomes the spark to ignite endeavour. In this context sin is understood not so much as a 'fall' as a failure to fulfil our potential according to the ability which is within us.

In the Hebrew mind, however, it is the otherness of God, His transcendence, which is the very basis of creation, and man's creative power is God's own gift. Here the Fall is not the wresting of secrets withheld, but the loss of right relationship whereby man's endeavour is turned toward self and to the neglect both of God and of neighbour. Equally it is this otherness of God which then becomes the very basis of hope in His ongoing creative purpose, through which man's creativity and skill are not so much restored as brought to their fulfilment, which fulfilment is also social in its affirmation of the worth of others. If indeed for the Classical mind 'to work is to pray', which is to be in tune with the creative power which is within one, for the Hebrew mind to work is to declare the glory of God, Whose whole creation (including mankind) is His 'handiwork'. Thus the otherness of God is not at the expense of His relationship to His world but is an integral part of it. And more especially it is this very sense of God's otherness which gives the Hebrew mind a particularly holistic outlook on life in the understanding of technology and of human creativity and endeavour, and as the setting withal of the marketplace.

Whilst this holistic perspective passed into Christianity from its Semitic roots, strangely it began to break apart at the Reformation (if not before). Certainly the Reformation turned the Church toward a particular appreciation of endeavour in the world and of the significance of the marketplace. Admittedly it moved the value of work from a kind of second-class activity (necessary, but inferior to the pursuit of the religious quest as such) to the status of a calling in its own right. So Luther interpreted Ecclesiasticus 11.21 'Trust in the Lord and abide in thy *labour*' (A.V. translation; N.E.B. = 'job') as 'Beruf' i.e. as vocation or calling. But this appreciation of the place of work and of the marketplace was at a price. In the case of Lutheranism faith was expressed not so much as an act of the intellect by which God is known but as an act of the will, the response to the saving power of God. Thus the will is in a position of primacy over the intellect. Here we can begin to trace the emergence of some of the problems associated with the place of reason in the context of belief, an issue which has contributed not only to debate in the rise of the scientific method, but which also now affects the understanding of the world of work and of commerce, which world is also governed fundamentally by rational activity. Thus the separation of will from intellect, for all the appreciative rediscovery of the marketplace, led to the Church's inability in the long run to respond adequately to the claims of the marketplace, where these claims derive ultimately from rational principles.

In the case of Calvinism the result was even worse, for a tight boundary (of the elect) was drawn around the Church distancing it from the wider world of God's creation. What Calvin succeeded in doing, in the Reformed appreciation of the marketplace, was to link the elect Christian's virtue of hard work (prosperity being a sign of God's blessing) to the Medieval Church's virtue of obedience. Whilst undoubtedly cities such as Geneva and Edinburgh became thriving centres of commerce, once the religious principles which had undergirded this self confidence in the marketplace had evaporated, the Reformed tradition equally had little with which adequately to address the issues raised by the realities and possibilities of economic life.

Similarly other traditions, both Protestant and Catholic, have had to wrestle with these issues, especially as these have been focused through various understandings of the meaning and value of work. For example, Roman Catholic thinking has ranged from 'work' interpreted as a result of the Fall as 'toil', and thus being toil it is something to be endured as the lot of fallen man (Pope Leo XIII *Rerum Novarum* 1891), to 'work' as the means of creative self-improvement, which is perfectly in keeping with the plan of Divine Providence (Pope John Paul II *Laborem Exercens* 1981), to the scope of wealth creation in a free market economy (Pope John Paul II *Centesimus Annus* 1991 and a century on from *Rerum Novarum*). The development of Free Church thinking in England (including Methodism) recognised a dilemma whereby hard work was a virtue but the possibility of consequent wealth creation could undermine the values of faith. Thus Wesley, and others before him, (on the basis of such Scriptural texts as 1 Timothy 6.17-19) encouraged hard work combined with the necessity of giving wealth away for the benefit of wider society. It tended to be the case, however, that it was employers rather than employees who actually undertook such philanthropy. In the Anglican Communion, the Lambeth Conference of 1897, whilst affirming the honourable status of work, decried the unemployed as morally weak. By 1918 a Church of England Report had moved on sufficiently to call for the application of Christian values as much to economic industrial life as to personal conduct. The writings of William Temple subsequently, in the idea of 'social gospel', reminded the Church of the fundamental link between creative work and human fulfilment, and of the implications of this for community involvement and for the well-being of society as a whole. In more recent times the Churches, in broad ecumenical agreement, have pointed to the need to give attention to the quality of work, especially as that which expresses human dignity, and which as part of that worth must avoid a materialism which denies the aspirations of others and which, unchecked, will despoil the planet.

Such a range of attitudes, and in some cases a shift in attitude, demonstrates a dilemma now upon the Church in reassessing the marketplace as a fact of people's lives and the control which it exerts over our lives. Looking back one cannot help feeling that, at least in the West, the distancing of the will from reason in the religious understanding of the day (particularly in Protestantism) actually contributed to a fragmentation of matter from spirit. This allowed a perspective of the Market gradually to evolve in which the wider material world became effectively placed outside the realm of religion. Yet in light of a century of rapid change (amongst the greatest in human history), and the consequences for the material well-being of all people, there is great need for the Church to reflect in new ways on its belief in God as Creator/Artisan and on the possibility of affirming (to use Charles Williams' phrase) the 'co-inherence' of *all* human activity in the transcendent.[2]

In one sense of course the Church has never left the marketplace in so far as the laity in general earn their living and have their livelihood there. Yet the Church has given little attention to, concern for, and support of Christians in their actual working lives. Stipendiary clergy may have little understanding (in the nature of their being stipendiary) of the possibilities and the pressures of secular work, (and in the case of the unemployed the lack of work), even if they, no less than others, may institutionally and personally feel the influence of market forces.

It is in part the response of the Church in its wish to be in touch more fully with the life of the laity in the world, including the world of work and of the marketplace, which has led to the emergence of a pattern of non-stipendiary ministry described variously as Worker-Priest, Secular Clergy, or (as the commonest expression in the Church of England) Minister in Secular Employment (MSE). The tributaries that have fed into this particular stream of ministry are various, some going back a considerable way. Amid the varied patterns of ministry evident within the Church, Ministry in Secular Employment might appear to be a particular development emerging from the diversity of Non-Stipendiary Ministry (NSM) in general. Yet in origin it would be more true to say that MSE was very much the pioneering vision that led to the possibility of a non-stipendiary ministry in the first place. This original vision of a work-focused ministry has since (and for some not without misgivings) been overtaken by, if not lost amongst, a wider (predominantly parish-focused, post retirement) ministry, leaving the original vision of a Ministry in Secular Employment as something of a remnant. (Currently only 20 per cent of all Non-Stipendiary Ministers are work-focused clergy.) If this particular view of the broad development of NSM is taken, it could be difficult to reply to the charge that NSM is primarily the result of market forces taking hold within the Church generally, in light of the decline in membership and income, and the continuing need nonetheless for ordained clergy. At any rate the focus of a self-supporting ministry addressed to the specific scope of secular employment continues to represent an attempt by the Church to understand anew and to address the complexities of secular employment—which after all is the broad experience one way or another of the membership of the Church.

The origins of MSE are comparatively recent though reference may be made to evidence linking ministry and secular employment almost from the very beginning. On closer examination, however, the bulk of this evidence is not so much about addressing ministry in secular employment as illustrative of the ways by which clergy have resorted to secular employment to supplement income and thus maintain themselves in the ministry. Particular reference will often be made to St. Paul, who was by trade a tent-maker/leather worker—a useful trade in terms of its portability and adaptability to different locations, and its being in regular demand, even though it undoubtedly entailed long hours for only a modest income. Paul makes a number of references to his employment, though the reasons for his choosing a self-supporting ministry are unclear. He could have accepted the right which others (e.g. Peter) claimed to be supported by the church, in keeping with the interpretation of a saying of Jesus '..the labourer deserves his food' (Matt.10.10, Luke 9.4 and 10.7 cf. 1 Cor. 9.13-14). The model of a self-supporting ministry is however testified to in Jewish Rabbinic tradition, and provides probably the best explanation of Paul's practice[3] (cf Pirqe Aboth 2.2 'Rabban Gamaliel (the 3rd) the son of Rabbi Judah the prince said—an excellent thing is the study of the Torah combined with some worldly occupation...').[4] But to claim that Paul was a kind of prototype Minister in Secular employment is rather misleading. Paul's references to his work are made not with reference to the *context* of his preaching but to the means of income support that enabled him, with a measure of independence, to conduct his missionary work in the founding of churches. So far as we can tell, this was the real context of his ministry, which is confirmed by the fact that when the Philippians made a gift to him which enabled him to give up his work and devote himself full-time to the ministry of the churches in his care (2 Cor.11.7-10 and Phil.4.15-17) he accepted it.

The origins of Ministry in Secular Employment (that is as the specific aim of the Church to respond to the issues and challenges of work and paid employment) may be traced most particularly in this century to the vision of F.R. Barry, (Bishop of Southwell), who in the 1930's expressed a call for the involvement of the ordained ministry in the secular life of the world. (In this Barry was influenced in part by the idea of 'voluntary clergy' advocated by Roland Allen, which was a wider plea for clergy to be more generally sponsored from within, and therefore in closer touch with, the life of the laity in the local church setting.) Thus:

> The secular tasks of the world are integral elements in the life of the Church, and involved in the service of its altars. Else holiness is a word with no meaning.... The family, the professions and Council Chambers, the technical skill on which modern life depends, are not merely fields for experiment in which to test our loyalty to the Church. They are themselves the material of Churchmanship. That is to say, it is not merely a question of carrying religion out into life amid the temptations of the world. It is a question of doing the world's work and responding to its opportunities with insight cleansed and motive directed by the grace of God through Jesus Christ.

And again:

> The real strength of the case is one of principle. It is the desire to exhibit the Ministry as the consecration and focus of the ministry of the whole Christian body in the normal activities of life.... What would it not mean to the Christian Group if the ministrant of God's gift for the sanctification of its Christian ministry were one who was actually sharing in the

tasks and temptations of 'secular' daily life, and were looked up to as its natural leader in the life of Christian citizenship and service? Nor can one think of any experiment which, while preserving the Christian emphasis on the 'givenness' of the means of Grace, as symbolised in a duly ordained Ministry, would do so much to safeguard the Church against the dominance of the clerical mind. It would help very effectively to demonstrate the sacramental character of the Church and the priestly vocation of the Christian life. It is on these essentially catholic grounds that the suggestion ought to be put forward.... The suggestion violates no catholic principle: it involves merely a change in accepted custom and a partial revision of apostolic practice.[5]

The process of recognition of Ministry in Secular Employment slowly gathered momentum by a blend of experiment and discussion, being finally agreed (by the Church of England) in February 1987. But in the contemporary setting, what aims and ideas might inform this ministry, particularly where this is exercised within the world of business, commerce or industry, that is within the daily life of the marketplace? The context of Christian ministry is both the secular world and the worshipping community, but the kind of ministry characterised by Ministry in Secular Employment is not about the traditional way in which these two, Church and society, have been understood i.e. the work of the minister as building up the body of Christ so that 'they', the laity, might work and witness effectively in the world. Rather it is about the sense of being in the world, believed to be God's world, in which clergy and laity together may celebrate and explore the scope of the Gospel as this arises within the opportunities and issues of working life itself. The ordained minister who exercises his or her ministry in the work-place is an accredited representative of the Church and as such is a sign and symbol of the Church's concern for the world. Such ministry, shared with the laity, derives from the sacramental nature of God's Presence present not only within the community of worship but also within the community of work which is gathered for the purposes of work. To ask if e.g. ordained clergy are actually needed in this way to undertake Christian ministry in the work setting, or whether this ordained ministry will rob the laity of their own rightful ministry—such questions as these betray the assumption of a traditional under-standing of the role of the clergy, as the full-time (professional) stipendiaries who 'send the laity out' to their work in the world. This is not to say that stipendiary parish clergy are not a necessary part of the Church. But there is a need for an increase in Ministry in Secular Employment if the Church is not to be relegated to becoming a cult community, and if the world of work, commerce and industry is to be understood, at times challenged, and more generally affirmed by the Church.

In the skill (techne) of the potter and in his handiwork, Jeremiah, as we have seen, discerned the handiwork of God. For Judaism, and subsequently for Christianity with its God-world relationship described as incarnational, the holy and the secular are inter-related. That is to say the secular is capable of receiving holiness and does not necessarily exclude the holy. One says 'not necessar-ily' because there are of course times when all is not right. Wrong, sin or whatever we call it, has a power to disrupt, corrupt and even, to use a market image, bankrupt. Yet by God's grace (that is by His being Creator and Redeemer) the created order may and will forever participate in the holiness of God. That is part at least of what Christians affirm in the Resurrection of Christ, the worship of God which acknowledges and celebrates the undying and undeniable worthship that the world has in the will and purpose of God. In this sense the world in its secularity is also holy, not by acquiring some new power of its own, but by being held by, re-established through, and brought to completion in a right relation-ship with God.

With this kind of undergirding theological framework, the Minister in Secular Employment shares with the laity two import-ant dimensions which distinguish him or her from both stipendiary and indeed sector ministry colleagues such as industrial chap-lains—the MSE is himself not a visitor to but an employee/ employer within the world of work, and the MSE may also thereby make of his ministry (as the laity do) a voluntary offering. Of course it is important to recognise that the stipendiary minister is not paid for his ministry but is paid to enable him to exercise his ministry. Yet the MSE, who is in the nature of the case non-stipendiary, is much closer to the circumstances of the laity. By virtue of their secular employment many of these ministers will be bound up in a variety of ways with the issues of the marketplace directly. It would not be surprising that on occasion their appreciation of these issues may be in tension with those of their stipendiary colleagues, and in some cases may actually provide a necessary corrective to them.

This combination of being both employee and 'volunteer' may seem a contradiction, but in the scope of a common basis of shared ministry between MSE and laity it represents an important expression of faith. The status of employee (or employer or self-employed) is for the MSE the recognition of the need to earn a livelihood and of the reality of economic forces; the style of the voluntary represents what would be recognised (in traditional terms) as a kind of stewardship, of offering, including the making of an offering of one's (work-place) life-setting to God.[6] This is more than, and in the end different from, company loyalty. Morale may be important, and loyalty, commitment and diligence even more so, in company terms, for the well-being literally of the business, but the role of the MSE and the lay person will be more than affirming good personal relationships in terms of management style. It will certainly include that but it will be more than that. What might this 'more' be understood to mean?

This 'more' is very much to do with a sense of the transcendent which we have already referred to, and about a wish to recover and acknowledge the transcendent at the heart of life. And this has everything to do with the marketplace—not in the sense of saying that there is more to life than work, nor in the sense even of saying that people are more than consumers (though there is profound truth in such claims). If God is more than ourselves, in the sense of other than/greater than ourselves, then the acknowledgement of Him as Creator, in the unfolding of Jeremiah's image of Artisan/Craftsman, is the very basis of our creative responsibility. And it is this creative purpose at the heart of life which should actually release us from wanting more and more in a selfish acquisitive sort of way, and which should turn us toward discovering an understanding of 'more' as a dimension to life which is inclusive and including—that is, an understanding of the Market in the context of community. In Christian terms it is to set (to use two Greek words from the New Testament) 'oikonomia' in the context of 'oikoumene'. 'Oikonomia' is about the flourishing of community which (in the context of 'oikoumene' i.e. the wider scene, the world at large) is not only for the success of the company and the benefit of the shareholders and employees, but also for the part that is played in the social scheme of things. In saying this one is not saying that the aim of business is social welfare, but it is to remind us of the possibility of the general good which paradoxically (because of the necessity of the Market) is sustained through self-interest. Self-interest is not in this case necessarily selfishness. Business, commerce and industry in order to flourish require to have regard to their profitability and development, but it is the Church's particular responsibility to remind us all of the transcendent at the heart of life, our worthship, so that the inter-linking of profitability and service can be both maintained and understood.

In the New Testament (especially in the Jewish Christianity represented by Matthew and the Letter of James) there is condemnation of trading for gain where that has become or is used as an expression of selfishness.[7] But this is not the same as the necessity for profitability. Human beings being what they are, and corporate institutions also being what they are, it is of course possible for profitability to become aggrandizement, but it need not necessarily be so. There is accordingly a particular purpose for the Church, not in alienating itself by simply warning of the limitations of the Market, but in enabling all whose livelihood is in trade and industry to continue to see, or to discover/rediscover the wider 'common-wealth' in the fostering of a sense of 'oikoumene'.

In keeping with this sense of profitability which actually, when properly managed, can support the wider good, one could interpret 'more' as 'increase', a word which has a particular significance in the context of faith (as expressive of the widening purpose of God e.g. Isaiah 9.7, John 3.30). Thus the 'authority' of the Market in the root sense of the word (as 'augeo'—'enlarge, increase') might, and indeed should, address the wider inclusive nature of profitability.

A former Archbishop of Canterbury (perhaps recalling earlier days of learning New Testament Greek) once said that God's favourite prepositions were 'in' and 'through' rather than 'out of' and 'around'. What then might Ministry in Secular Employment, in the recollecting and nurturing of the 'transcendent' as 'more', contribute in the context of work, industry and commerce? Let me suggest three possibilities.

- Firstly such a ministry should seek to encourage in others a sense of 'flow' which is expressive of who we ourselves are, so that a sense of worth, meaning and purpose has relevance across the whole of life. To live in a non-compartmentalised way, so that work and involvement in life outwith work are not completely separated, is to begin to be open to a sense of the transcendent whereby one explores who one is, in the worth of who one is, within the totality of who one is. Business itself can recognise this and respond to it. So e.g. a recent recruitment brochure for a company declares that 'it is in our interest as well as yours to support and value the whole person'. And a notable statement from British Gas declares that 'the health of any business is dependent on the health of any community it serves'.[8] It has to be admitted that the Christian Church has not itself been particularly good at enabling the laity to relate faith to life and especially to work. More certainly needs to be done to address the diffidence of people in the worthwhileness of their insights and experience, and to encourage a greater 'flow' of being, and of integration, across and within the commitment, responsibilities and opportunities of life.

■ Secondly such a ministry might seek to remind colleagues that in the economy of the marketplace there is scope for meeting needs as well as responding to demands. Resources tend to be attracted to those sectors of the economy where there is demand, but should there not also be space to respond to what may in fact be needed? This is not necessarily to predetermine what should be provided, but it is to suggest a wider context for provision in a way which does not depart from a market economy. In some cases demand may enable need to be met at one and the same time e.g the extension of a pipeline (in response to a 'demand') may enable some worthwhile conservation to be provided (as a 'need') in the process. But there may be possibilities (and in fact almost all major manufacturing industries in this country respond in some way with investment to this) of meeting certain needs in the community at large quite independently of the actual consumer demands of the market itself. Whilst such company support or sponsorship may not be entirely altruistic, it provides fruitful meeting points between business and social interests which are worth reflecting on as models of creative inter-relationship. This kind of opportunity (or to use a New Testament expression—'kairos') may offer some scope for what one might call the creative exploitation of randomness. One says exploitation, rather than exploration, for it may in fact be just that. And this calls for a particular re-combining of reason and will. The world of work, as we have already noted, is essentially rational, with defined objectives, job descriptions and spread sheets. On the other hand the Market itself is frequently fluid, and even (perhaps) at times chaotic. Of course that leaves opportunity for exploitation (in a selfish way) and a quick profit (or loss) for people who take a risk. But in a wider way opportunities can arise which, if the vision is there, can harness resources to meet particular needs—and if the will is there, combined with the reasonableness of possibility, these needs can be met within the aims and structures of commercial enterprise itself. The Church should be more involved than it is, within the setting of the work-place itself, in discussing ways by which benefit may be actually and actively a part of profit.

- Thirdly such a ministry should foster a sense of corporate self-esteem which, seen almost as the weaving of a company's 'story', provides a statement which is more than a statement told in profit and loss curves or in exchange rates. An institution which whilst paying the wage or salary of its employees places the emphasis on people's productivity rather than on the worth-whileness of their contribution (in whatever form of skill that may express itself) will really tend toward an impersonal view of corporate structures—so people will become a rather mechanistic 'company resource'. To enable people to feel valued in whatever role they have should be a first claim on a company's purpose. And this may be helped by reflecting upon the undertaking as a whole, as the 'story' told to itself of its planning and self-involving purpose—*not* as superficial glossy publicity but as a true exploration of corporate endeavour. In this employer and employee might feel more mutually participant and see in a more sustained way the links between community in work, and life in the wider community of which they are also a part. This is not to advocate, by other means, the recent concept of Total Quality Management (BS5750) in Business and Commerce, whose aim is 'to seek to win the hearts and minds of the workforce to provide total quality and service to our customers'. In the end one suspects that such values may be another device to subsume 'service' to profitability whereby both employee and customer are means to an end.[9] Whatever be the necessity for profit, a sense of 'quality' as a business value must ensure that employees are not manipulated to sustain output, and that the creativity of public life, which in the end is larger than the marketplace, is not subverted by consumption. In this interpretative process a sense of 'narrative' theology, applied to the circumstances of working life, can be a useful way in which Ministry in Secular Employment may engage fully with the enterprise of work and, if it is not too much to say this, be open to the Presence of God not only alongside but from the side of colleagues in secular life.

In exploring such themes as these the Minister in Secular Employment might find that there really is less of a gap between the creativity of work with all its related social significance and the creativity of faith.

Notes

1 Cupitt, D., *Christ and the Hiddenness of God*, SCM, 1985, p. 16.

2 See especially Williams, Charles, *The Image of the City and Other Essays*, Anne Ridler (ed), Oxford University Press, 1958, pp. 102-111.

3 There is evidence from the Greek Cynic tradition of self-supporting teachers and philosophers. See especially Hock, Ronald F., *The Social Context of Paul's Ministry (Tent-Making and Apostleship)*, Fortress Press, 1980.

4 Translation from *The Jewish Prayer Book*, Singer, S., 'The Ethics of the Fathers', *ad loc.*

5 Barry, F.R., *The Relevance of the Church*, Nisbet, 1935, Chapter 6, p. 213ff; For the ideas presented by Roland Allen (1868-1947) see his *The Case for Voluntary Clergy*, Eyre and Spottiswoode, 1930. The development of the idea of Ministry in Secular Employment in this country has emerged gradually and by a different route from a pattern in France known as the Worker Priest Movement. That began during and after the second World War as a deliberate involvement on the part of the Church in working life, a movement which was re-established as the Mission de France in 1954. In England the preferred direction was that of Industrial Chaplaincy. This pattern continues in the Church as an important expression of sector ministry. It has clear points of contact with Ministry in Secular Employment, but is also fundamentally different in its non work-employee status.

6 See e.g. Charles Wesley's hymn 'Forth in thy Name O Lord I go, my daily labour to pursue.'

7 Matt.5.19-20 cf.5.24b 'You cannot serve God and Mammon'; James 5.1-3 cf.4.13 'Today or tomorrow we will go into such and such a town and spend a year there and trade and get gain.' The reference to rust in Matt.6.20 and James 5.3 is a play on the contrasted colour of gold.

8 'How British Gas Helps the Community', *Student Industrial Society*, 1991, p. 8.

9 See the discussion in *The Newsletter Amongst Ministers at Work*, No. 40 December 1991, (editorial), p.1; and No. 41, March 1992, reply by Ian Wilson, pp. 7-8.

Selling God—
A Job for Commercial Television?

Vin Arthey

Introduction

In this paper I discuss two general and one specific area of interest in religious broadcasting in the UK. I deal with the history and development of religious broadcasting as a whole and then with the specific market within which religious broadcasting has developed since the advent of commercial television. I look in particular at ITV's religious series, 'Morning Worship', and at the current concerns in that programme of both its producers and its consumers. The nineteenth century Cuban patriot said of his years in the USA that 'I know the monster, I have lived in its entrails'. I know the TV monster—I work in its entrails!

The Development of Religious Broadcasting in the UK

The history of broadcasting really began at the time of the First World War, when radio was used for transmitting military orders across considerable distances. Unfortunately, anyone with a receiver could pick up the messages, with the consequent operational dangers. But for immediate communication with large numbers of people it was ideal. The modern idea of *broadcasting* was born.

Religious programmes were among the first to be broadcast by the BBC in the 1920s, largely because the first manager of the BBC, John Reith, was a staunch Christian determined to imbue his company with that faith. In those days, of course, the power of the Church in the State was much greater than it is now. Many of Reith's early radio programmes were *talks* on religious and moral subjects, but there was also a 'Daily Service' (continued to this day), a Sunday worship programme broadcast live from a church location, and much broadcasting of religious music.

Some of the very first BBC television programmes in the 1930s were religious programmes, and when British commercial television began in the 1950s, the ITV regions all transmitted regular Sunday worship programmes.

The British experience of television was not unique, as live broadcasts of religious programmes were a feature of early Dutch and Swedish television. British television as a whole, however, received a special boost with the live coverage of Queen Elizabeth's coronation—itself a largely religious affair. For many Britons, this was the occasion to buy or rent a television set.

Three things emerge out of this brief history. First, British broadcasting legislation between the 1920s and the 1980s had no *requirement* whatever for religious broadcasting. Religious programmes existed because of strong official and popular cultural support. Secondly, making worship programmes is very demanding, but both professionally rewarding and very enjoyable. Thirdly, it is cheap! Neither clergy nor laity demand huge fees for appearing, and premises are usually freely available.

Commercial Television and Religious Broadcasting in the 1990s

From the 1950s to the late 1980s, ITV had in effect a monopoly of television advertising and in that sense did not operate in a real market. The development of cable television and the more recent satellite channels have broken the monopoly and totally altered the lives of all those who work in the industry. The Conservative government, concerned in this as in other industries to introduce genuine competition, made sure that regional TV licences to sell airtime went to companies which were both broadcasters of quality and financially sound. The 'bidding' process was presided over by the Independent Television Commission (the ITC), and most of the fifteen regional licences which were awarded went to licencees who chose to be both programme *makers* as well as broadcasters. The largest of these companies make most of the network programmes. The ITC is required to supervise 'with a light touch', but paradoxically perhaps at the very moment of deregulation came, for the first time, the requirement that the ITV companies broadcast religious programmes *by law*.

An in-depth analysis of this requirement has yet to be made, but it seems clear that the Government was at the time concerned about the scandals involving certain American 'televangelists'. The UK Government prohibited religious groups from holding licences but at the same time showed a positive response to the religious lobbies. It was also able to demonstrate its view that Channel 3 was a 'quality' channel. On one reading of this saga, it would seem that the Government's view of religion was very much tied up in the ideas about heritage—'Britain's Religious Heritage'—and it is certainly the case that 'Heritage' plays a large part in the profile of the Conservative Government. The Minister responsible for broadcasting and the arts in general is the Secretary of State for National Heritage.

The new licensing system began in January 1993. As far as religious programmes are concerned there will be little change. The ITC requires the network to put out *two hours* of religious programmes per week, of which one hour is likely to be a worship programme. The ITC cannot dictate where in the weekly schedule such programmes should appear. The licence granted to Tyne Tees for the North East commits the company to transmit the equivalent of twelve minutes of religious programmes per week in addition to the network requirement.

Financial Implications

How are these programmes to be paid for? *Regional* programmes are simply a cost to the company—there is no return. The programmes are made, as are news programmes, as part of the licence requirement. The money to pay for such programmes comes from the selling of air time to advertisers, the main source of company revenue.

Network programmes of all sorts (such as drama, situation comedy, documentaries) are paid for by contributions from every ITV company to a network fund or pool. The contribution varies according to the size of the company. The network then buys programmes from the programme makers, at set prices, and pays for them out of the pool.

Network religious programmes are paid for with money from this pool. To take Tyne Tees Television as an example: the company is a maker and supplier of a half a dozen or so live 'Morning Worship' programmes a year, a similar number of 'Highway' (the religious light entertainment show with Sir Harry Secombe), and a few minutes of religious documentary material. Some of the 'Highway' programmes are also sold overseas. In percentage terms (the actual figures are naturally confidential) religious programmes account for 10 per cent of Tyne Tees' income from programme sales, compared with drama, 61 per cent, and quiz programmes, 14 per cent. In terms of hours supplied, religious programmes account for 12 per cent, quizzes 38 per cent, drama 15 per cent—drama is expensive, quiz programmes are cheap! The six 'Morning Worship' programmes will bring in about half the income of the 'Highway' programmes.

'Morning Worship' is televised worship, broadcast live from selected religious venues. A list is drawn up of venues on the basis of a national ratio of Christian denominations, two Anglican for one Roman Catholic and one mainline Free Church. Surplus Sundays are allocated to 'minority' Free Churches and to the Orthodox Church. The 'live' format has been an ITC requirement. Network policy on 'Morning Worship', in the formulation of which Tyne Tees was very much involved, is based upon the idea of a 'typical' service to be found anywhere within the British Isles. The broadcasters visit the chosen Church as guests and as a community of broadcasters transmit the worshipping community's service to the viewing community. The policy is underpinned by a British Christian tradition and by a commitment to freedom of worship in a tolerant, pluralistic society.

At the moment there is an audience for 'Morning Worship' of between 350,000 and one million people. This compares with, say, 'Coronation Street's' audience of 16 million—or with the BBC2 arts programme, 'The Late Show's' audience of 300,000. 'Morning Worship' has a high 'Appreciation Index' of 80 per cent plus, higher than the ratings for sports or situation comedy programmes.

In terms of internal costs, 65 per cent of the production costs of 'Morning Worship' are taken up with staff salaries and facilities, as compared 55 per cent on the same items for the company as a whole. Of the remainder, 13 per cent of the cost of 'Morning Worship' comes from equipment hire (generators, for example) and 9 per cent on staff expenses.The only item of expenditure where 'Morning Worship' is cheaper than the company average for network programmes as a whole is on payments to outside participants, ie. facility fees for churches, preachers and music costs. The higher than average costs are due to the *live, outside* broadcast policy.

The Future for Religious Broadcasting

The pressure is on cost, that is to say on the 'live element'. Services could be recorded and transmitted on tape. It would be possible to record a 'batch' of services, all from one location. A church, a redundant church perhaps, could be acquired and 'wired', with a fixed lighting rig and imported congregations. A studio could stand in for a church. How, one wonders, would such practices affect the liturgy and theology of worship, or the experience of the television audience? What is a recorded Eucharist? The issue of recorded services has liturgical and theological implications, as well as financial and televisual ones: and it is certainly a topic much under discussion at the moment.

Conclusion

It is, obviously, not television's job to save souls: that is clearly the job of the church. ITV *sells* airtime and programmes, and is obliged to maximise audience size and profits. Yet there has for seventy years now been a tradition of religious broadcasting in this country. Both BBC and ITV provide a mixed and varied schedule, and television is arguably the most important medium through which we celebrate and talk to each other in our society. Religion is as much part of our culture as (at least!) sport, light entertainment, the arts, drama, politics etc., and its future needs as serious a debate as the future of all of those.

From the IEA Health & Welfare Unit

Saving Lives: The NHS Accident and Emergency Service and How to Improve It

Miles Irving et. al. £5.95 34pp

More than 1,000 people die every year in Britain because of the failure of accident and emergency services, according to a report published today
The Times

At least 1000 people die unnecessarily every year ... [the authors] describe their claim as conservative. **Daily Telegraph**

The growing acceptance that health cash is limited should lead to concentration on services for younger patients that show proven results in restoring people to active life, the report argues **The Guardian**

Casualty bungles kill 1000 **Today**

Empowering the Parents: How to Break the Schools Monopoly

David Green et. al. £6.95 90pp

The IEA, founded in 1955, has published pamphlets and papers that questioned the post-war orthodoxies in economics and welfare. ... the notions of choice, of independent schools and institutions, and of competition between them are unlikley to go away
British Journal of Educational Studies

Good teachers have to be set free from the dead weight of politicans and town hall bureaucrats, says the Institute of Economic Affairs.
Liverpool Daily Post

Good teachers must be set free from the dead weight of politicians and town hall bureaucrats, the Institute of Economic Affairs said in a report.
Independent

Also from the IEA Health & Welfare Unit

Equal Opportunities: A Feminist Fallacy
Caroline Quest et. al.   £6.95   **111pp**

The authors argue that all equality legislation should be abolished so that the free market can operate without any restraint   **The Independent**

Laws banning sex discrimination and promoting equal pay at work damage the intersts of women the Institute of Economic Affairs claims today   **Daily Telegraph**

Let us not above all be politically correct. Let us not become overheated because the Institute of Economic Affairs has brought out a startling report entitled Equal Opportunities: A Feminist Fallacy.   **The Times**

Laws which effectively promote "preferential hiring" policies "harm women" according to an essay in a recent book from the Insitute of Economic Affairs   **Industrial Relations Review and Report**

Families without Fatherhood
N Dennis & G Erdos   £7.95   **127pp**

The British equivalent of America's anti-welfare manifesto may now have been written by ... Dennis and Erdos   **The Sunday Times**

Boys brought up in one-parent families without a father are more likely to turn to anti-social behaviour, varying from unruliness to street rioting   **Daily Telegraph**

the report ... focuses on the decline of fatherhood rather than the usual moralising about one-parent families ... and [breaks] through both left and right knee-jerk responses   **The Guardian**

a new book published by (provactively) ... the IEA   **The Economist**

Rising crime, riots and violence were linked to the subsequent increase in the number of fatherless families   **The Times**

Also from the IEA Health & Welfare Unit

Undermining Innovation: Parallel Trade in Prescription Medicines

M Burstall & I Senior   £12.95   76pp

The pricing issue, of increasing concern to the industry, is highlighted by a report today from the ... Institute of Economic Affairs.   **Daily Telegraph**

The European Communities single market has generated some curious trade distortions, none more so than one in the drugs industry.
Financial Times

Their report ... assesses the scale of parallel importing and examines a range of possible changes, at national and EC level, that could effects the pricing and profitability of the pharmaceutical industry.   **Scrip**

Working Class Patients and the Medical Establishment

David Green   £9.95   211pp HB

a unique study of the development of the relationship between producers and consumers of primary medical care in the hundred years up to the creation of the National Health Service... a well documented historical study   **Political Quarterly**

a fascinating analysis of the actual workings of medicine under the friendly societies... Market competition actually served the needs of the people well   **New Society**

an important, if controversial, contribution   **Sociology**

**By far the best and cheapest way to obtain IEA Health and Welfare Unit books is to take out an annual subscription.
For further details contact the Health and Welfare Unit on (071) 799 3745**